ERIC CARROLL

...AND JUSTICE FOR DADS

THE FORGOTTEN PARENT IN FAMILY COURT

ASHMAN FREE PRESS

To request permissions, contact the publisher at
danielashman@protonmail.com

ISBN: 978-1-962192–08-8 (Paperback)
ISBN: 978-1-962192–10-1 (Hardback)
ISBN: 978-1-962192–09-5 (eBook)
ISBN: 978-1-962192-11-8 (Audio)

First print edition September 2024

AFP

ASHMAN FREE PRESS
Boston, MA
AshmanFreePress.com

*This is dedicated to the greatest dad of them all
—my father.*

CONTENTS

I Stand With John.

Nov. 5, 1980 - Feb 5, 2021 (age 40)

∾

For I know the plans I have for you declares the Lord, plans to prosper you and not to harm you, plans to give you hope and a future. Jeremiah 29:11

THE MURDER OF JOHN MAST

BY ROBERT MAST

My son, John Mast, was born in 1980 in Ohio.

John grew up in a quiet rural atmosphere where he absorbed the values of our mostly Amish culture and religion. This provided him with the solid ethic of honor, and virtuous character traits that marked his entire life journey, even as we evolved into a more mainline "Jesus is our Lord" life.

He married Becky at the age of 28 and a few years later they relocated from our Northwest Montana area to Williston, North Dakota where he secured a stable year-round delivery job. In '12 and '13 Ashira and Zayne were born. John applied himself fully to being a good father as well as a good husband, but by then, we realized Becky was not sound mentally.

In early '17 she overdosed on prescription meds and I think John saved her life by getting her to the hospital rapidly upon finding her unconscious. But we were dismayed that she did not totally follow through on her needed mental care. Ten months later she alleged John physically assaulted her, but the video from the restaurant where it allegedly happened, clearly exonerated him. She took out a restraining order so John couldn't be a part of his children's lives except for short supervised visits. John soon filed and was given full interim custody, but Becky didn't easily cooperate, and when he finally did get the children, within 6 days, she made false sexual allegations against him. This resulted in the kids being taken and placed in foster care, and several months later, placed in her care. The next evil poison used against John was Becky alienating the kids from Dad.

Finally, in Dec of '20 the judge released the custody order, it gave John the kids on the next two holidays, but she refused to comply. Then came the fateful day of February 5th. John was supposed to have the kids for the weekend. He went to the Rosauer's parking lot and waited to pick up his kids. Becky's car pulled in, parked, and out of the car got Becky's father who took out a gun and shot and killed John.

The family courts often fail, but the greater failure was the CPS response, and then the court not being timely in our case.

There is a crisis here in our country that fathers are often removed from their God-given role in their children's lives. It needs to be exposed so we the people can become involved in bringing correction.

We need to understand that from the very beginning of time God instituted marriage between one man and one woman, with children as God's creation in this union. He mandated both parents as having the responsibility to love, teach and train them into adulthood. There is no other plan that has a high success rate.

Father's rights are not prioritized in our society today. There is a bias in many quarters against fathers. I see failures all too often when the marriage union fails: no timely court response, family court judges lacking knowledge and understanding, no punishment of women committing perjury, and many Child Protective Services failures.

These deficiencies are often forerunners to violence, child abuse and death. We can and must do better than this.

The very worst weapons that are used today are false sexual allegations and parental alienation.

This is where Eric Carroll excels. He has been many years recording the worst situations, and often getting involved to help the most abused by the system. Read carefully all he has to offer. Be aware and find your part in saving our most valuable resource—our children. Eric has much to offer to bring corrections to these problems.

In loving memory of Sophia Larson.

May 5, 2014 - December 11, 2019 (age 5)

SOPHIA'S STORY

BY ALEC LARSON

I affiliated myself with the older crowd in high school. This group of people is where I met Stephanie. She was everything I wanted as a 15 year old boy. She was older, had the looks and was always ready to go out and party or have fun. I was hooked. I had Stephanie, and, I had baseball. If I wasn't with Stephanie I was on the baseball diamond trying to find my way to a scholarship, and I was on my way. That is until the summer between my junior and senior year of high school when my life changed forever.

It was only a few weeks before I was to start my senior year of high school and make my big push to find a school that wanted me on their team when Stephanie came to me and told me she was pregnant. Pregnant! I was at a loss for words. I never returned to high school and my dreams of playing baseball ended. But I was excited, scared also but mostly excited. I began looking for work wherever I could get hired at 17 years old, so mostly fast food joints or temp services. It wasn't a lot but it was enough. I signed my first lease before we welcomed our baby girl into this world and before I was even 18 years old. On May 5th, 2014, six days before my 18th birthday, Sophia Jazlyn Larson was born. Seeing my daughter for the first time changed the way I thought, acted, worked, anything and everything about me became a man because of that little innocent baby girl. I knew I had made the right choice to focus on my new family instead of stay in school and risk not being in her life.

Sophia quickly grew into such a beautiful and smart little girl even at her young age. Sophia's soul was pure and innocent. She was the light in our family. Unfortunately Stephanie and I were growing apart. She was going back to the life we had before Sophia. Staying out all night, or just plum not coming home at all. I could see that there was something, or someone else that had Stephanie's attention. It wasn't long after Sophia's 4th birthday that I confronted Stephanie about our relationship trying to get answers as to why I felt like I was losing her. The conversation turned to an argument where she attacked me, punched me, and ended with me having a cut above my eye and my blood all over the bathroom. Stephanie left the house and took Sophia. I stayed at my mother's house for the night and decided Sophia was better off with parents separated than seeing what she witnessed the day before. Stephanie attacking me. I went back to the house and my suspicions were confirmed when I found another man in bed with Stephanie as I arrived. This made it an easy decision for me to pack all of my stuff and leave Stephanie. I moved in with my mom to get back on my feet and try to find a place for Sophia and I to live.

Separating with Stephanie had me paranoid of what

was to come. My parents had a very ugly divorce and custody battle over my sister and I so I knew I was going to do whatever I could to prevent Sophia from having to go through that same scenario. To my luck and Sophia's disappointment Stephanie decided to choose parties over her daughter. I had full custody of Sophia without the headache of family court. It was Sophia and I against the world. Nothing could stop us. She would never let us be bored. This five year old little girl was more than my daughter, she was my best friend and I wouldn't have it any other way. Sophia missed her mom though. She absolutely loved and adored her mother. I did my best to arrange times for Sophia to be with Stephanie but more often than not Stephanie would have other plans arise or would just plain and simple not show up. There were too many times to count that Sophia would sit at the window watching outside for hours waiting on her mom to pick her up. I watched Stephanie start to break her own daughter down with nothing more than being absent. I made the decision to not tell Sophia when her mom was "coming" to pick her up just due to the fact that she was so unreliable and was hurting Sophia. But when she did show up, I would pack her a bag and let her go be with her mother.

I could see that Stephanie was losing a lot of weight very fast. I thought it was drugs, I knew it was drugs. So I took it upon myself to talk with Stephanie's father and tell him my concerns for Stephanie and Sophia when she is around her. Unfortunately that was about all I could do other than making sure Sophia was close by as much as possible.

December 11th, 2019 is a day I'll never forget. In the

morning Sophia and I got ready for school and work. We took our morning walk to the local bus stop and then across town to school. I didn't have a vehicle at the time so we always had a lot of time spent together on walks to and from school. As she went in to her Kindergarten class I headed off to work. It was a normal day until I heard from Stephanie. She told me she was going to pick up Sophia from school and take her home for the night. For once she stayed true to her word. Little did I know that she had been fired early that morning for failing a drug test at work. She went to work at a children's dentist office so high on meth that her bosses drug tested her on the spot. She then proceeded to pick up two of her cousin and continue smoking meth through the day until she went to pick up Sophia. Sophia went home with her mother and her two family members where they continued to party and smoke meth with Sophia in the apartment. After a while Sophia went to bed. She always needs a bottle of water with her though. Mom didn't give her one. A few hours went by and Sophia woke up thirsty so she came back out of the room to find a water bottle. Stephanie and her cousins, still smoking meth watched Sophia drink out of a bottle of water that they had put Meth inside. My Sophia overdosed and passed away from Meth a little less than four hours later.

Everything I loved, my one rock, my best friend, my five year old daughter was ripped away from me that night by her own mother. I didn't know what to do or where to go. I was lost in a world of unknown. I went through the viewing silent. I couldn't afford anything so I had to dig the hole myself that I was to bury my baby in. I knew what happened and I knew who killed my daughter but I had to keep my head down and get through it all in silence so the police could do their investigations. Finally arrests were made and Stephanie and her cousins went to jail. That's when I met Eric Carroll. He saw my story and heard my voice. He let me come onto his show and express the pain and anger that I had to deal with everyday on my own. Without Eric I don't think Sophia's story would have gotten the recognition and coverage that it needed to ensure justice was served for Sophia.

WHY WRITE THIS BOOK?

PREFACE

I never set out to be a podcaster. I never set out to be an advocate. But sometimes a calling is thrust upon you when you really weren't looking for one.

Before I began my podcast, *Dad Talk Today*, I'd been a route driver. And unless you've driven a truck for long stretches at a time—all day, every day—you likely don't know just how mundane life gets between deliveries and pickups. To mitigate the boredom in my cab, I listened to podcasts. I loved them.

As luck would have it, I tore my ACL, and then later found myself jobless after the trucking company was forced to lay off staff. So, there I was lamenting my lot in life when the flash of inspiration hit—why don't I start my own podcast?!

I thought a podcast would be a productive way to vent some of my frustration at what I'd encountered in the family court system and how it was rigged against men. I can tell you there was an absurdity about going through the process. Maybe with a podcast, I reasoned, I'd find a few like-minded guys along the way. Boy, did I ever! After just a couple of episodes, my social media channels already had ten-thousand followers.

The first episode of *Dad Talk Today* hit in the fall of 2019 and was titled "Parental Alienation." It focused on divorce, custody, and how women will sometimes use children as weapons against their soon-to-be-ex spouse. I'd been through it myself. The subject really hit a nerve with a whole lot of dads, which to me was both a relief and a horror. I was relieved to now know for certain that I wasn't alone, that there were lots of other guys just like me having a tough time getting the courts to help them with their custody issues. But that was also what horrified me.

I'd once felt like I had nobody to talk to—feeling isolated and all alone. I had no money and the only thing keeping me alive was knowing my kids needed me. It seemed nobody understood what I was going through. There certainly was nothing in the mainstream media or in any television show about dad issues.

So, I launched the podcast, and wow, I'd apparently found a niche no one else had because *Dad Talk Today* took off. But it wasn't without detractors. I was actually criticized for calling it *Dad Talk Today*. There was an entire online movement telling me to take the "dad" out of *Dad Talk Today*. I'd talked to some of the dads who'd long been fighting the good fight and they told me I should rename the podcast, *Parent Talk*. I was like, "What in the world is going on here?!" The reason it's called *Dad Talk Today* is because I'm talking to the dads who have nowhere else to turn.

Those same dads told me society isn't empathetic

toward men, and that it's especially not empathetic toward dads. They warned me that if I talked to legislators I shouldn't mention "fathers' rights" because they wouldn't listen to me.

I ignored them and it's a good thing I did. Since that first episode of *Dad Talk Today*, I've met with legislators from every state in America and boldly brought up the rights of dads. I've spoken with political candidates, movie stars, and other Hollywood celebrities. Let me tell you, when I first launched the podcast, I busted my rear end to get those people as guests. But once they heard what I had to say, well, let's just say, I was stunned at how many of them had similar experiences with the family court system.

Dads just can't catch a break nowadays. When they battle custody issues they are often portrayed as, "Oh, these guys have a victim mentality, they're just feeling sorry for themselves." To which I silently scream, "No they're not!" These are real guys going through real issues. The guys who've been mentally and financially broken by the system are looking for solutions, which they can't find anywhere, and they're going to family law attorneys who are basically snakes disguised as advocates. They act like a counselor, "Sure, we'll talk to you," because they're charging by the hour. But what dads need is a place where they can realize, "I'm not alone." That's why I created *Dad Talk Today*.

I'm still amazed that I have candid conversations with celebrities, congressmen and congresswomen, senators, and other influential people. I mean, I'm just a dad from Georgia. But here's the thing, we may be of different races, different creeds, different levels of education, or different income levels, but every single one of the fathers I've met are unified—unified by one thing: the need to protect their kids and to be a part of their lives.

We've struck a chord, so now let's work toward leveling the playing field, making an impact, and spurring change for dads and their kids.

INTRODUCTION

"Fathers don't pay child support! Fathers aren't active in their children's lives! Fathers are deadbeats!"

Admit it, you've heard at least one of these statements. We all have. For years these have been the sort of rote stereotypes we've heard about non-custodial dads, and heck, even custodial dads, too. And a lot of people believe them. But the fact is, they are just slanderous lies. When it comes to most dads, they simply are not true. In my experience—and the numbers prove it—dads want to take care of their kids and will fight like hell to do it often at great harm to themselves.

The truth is, you'll find plenty of cases where it's the mother who lives down to those stereotypes. Check your state child support services agency and you'll find plenty of women listed among the "deadbeat" parents. As I've said many times, toxic moms are just as bad as absent dads.

But before we fall knee-deep into the marshy swamp of "tit for tat," let's make something clear—my goal isn't to disparage mothers and it's not to claim that all dads are paragons of virtue. They're not. Like most anything, there's good and bad on both sides. People are people and not every parent is Mike or Carol Brady. I'm not here to say "All moms do this..." or "All moms do that..." But what really gets under my skin is how the feminist movement and those who oppose fathers' rights can say anything they want about dads no matter how untrue or unfair it might be. They can speak as much as they want about motherhood and strong independent women, but if we do the same about fatherhood, somehow we're wrong. My goal, whether it's for this book, my podcast, or on my various social media pages, is to celebrate fatherhood and to raise awareness about some of the disparities in family law that have profoundly affected dads across America. Truth be told, I believe in the traditional nuclear family. In a perfect world, families would stay together. Sadly, though, the world isn't perfect, and neither are any of us.

There are great moms and great dads, and there are some, well, not so great moms and dads. I'd like to think family court judges try to separate the wheat from the chaff but all too often the scale of justice is weighted to favor the mother, regardless of circumstance.

Let me give you an example. Recently in Colleyville, Texas, a town near Fort Worth, there was a 14-year-old boy who'd been diagnosed with cancer. He lived with his mother, who had legal custody. His father had the standard visitation arrangement as provided by the court. The boy battled courageously for three years before the cancer spread aggressively and his condition took a turn for the worse. His father was then told his son had no more than a few weeks to live. Sadly, those weeks came during the mother's "vacation" time as outlined in the custody order, and despite his repeated requests to see him, the mother would not allow the father access to his son outside of his "normal" visiting days.

You can imagine how devastating this was. A man with a dying son had no legal right to visit him. The pain, frustration, and the soul-crushing sorrow was further compounded by an ex who was weaponizing her dying son out of sheer vindictiveness.

So, for this grieving father, there was but one thing to do —he went to court and requested an emergency hearing. He hoped a judge, seeing the gravity of the situation, and possessing some measure of compassion, would issue an order allowing him access to his boy.

That's exactly what happened.

Sort of.

The judge granted the father three one-hour visits per day for the two weeks the doctor said the son now had left to live. Given the son had but a couple of weeks left, the visitation order wasn't particularly generous or fair—especially since the son himself told a social worker he wanted to spend the same amount of time with his father as he did with his mother. But what could the father do? He took whatever time he could get with his son during those last dying days.

Still though, despite the court order, more than once the mother denied his visitation. Father's Day came and she only "allowed" the guy a few hours to see his son. The following weekend, the boy died.

There were two separate funerals—one held by Mom, and one held by Dad.

How cruel was that mother? How cruel was that judge —to limit a man's access to his dying son? And how fair was the legal process to either the father or his son?

By the way, for those wondering—the father had no history of abuse or bad domestic behavior. He was simply the victim of a flawed system biased against fathers. Also, the mother suffered absolutely no repercussions whatsoever for violating the temporary visitation order.

Men are at a decided disadvantage in the family courts.

The absurdity of the process for fathers in those courts can't be overstated. For many men, it's often a choice between being bankrupted by the legal fees it takes just to navigate the byzantine system or giving up access to their kids.

Imagine this scenario: A man is in a toxic relationship with an abusive woman with whom he has a beautiful daughter. Of course, when a relationship begins no one knows it might lead to controlling, abhorrent behavior. You fall in love, your endorphins are dancing, the sky is blue, the birds are chirping, and it's all unicorns and rainbows. No one wants to believe the magic will end in a barrage of ugliness, lawyers, courts, and the weaponization of children. But sometimes it does. And for that man, it did.

Once the relationship ended, his ex kept their daughter. She would often choose to hold back visitation or put strange conditions on it, like, "I'll allow her to visit and stay over at your house as long as I stay there, too." It was his ex's way of maintaining control over him. That sort of behavior is wrong on many levels, not the least of which is the harm it causes a child. But it's not uncommon.

As a father who loved his daughter, the guy knew he

could either tread water by arguing and get nowhere, or he could hire a lawyer. What choice did he have? The system really doesn't allow for anything else—not when one of the parents is combative. He made the only sensible choice—he went to a lawyer. However, as he'd quickly learn, when it comes to custody issues for a dad, nothing is ever as easy as it seems. Little did the guy know this would be an introduction to the flawed family court system and its systemic bias against men.

The first lawyer with whom he consulted said, "If you want to see your daughter then get back with your ex. You'll never win in court. You're a man."

Wow! Talk about an eye-opener.

Here the man had a lawyer—an experienced one with years practicing law in the family courts—telling him that men have no chance whatsoever in winning a case there. How bad must the system be when the lawyer's solution to a custody/visitation conflict is to reunite with an abusive ex?

Seriously.

So, the man passed on that solution and went to another lawyer. This one wanted ten-thousand dollars just to retain him, and as anyone who has ever hired a lawyer knows, it doesn't take long to go through the retainer before the legal fees really start adding up. At that time, the guy couldn't afford it. So, he went in search of some sort of legal aid but found there wasn't a single resource for non-custodial men. Not one.

What a horrible experience for a man just trying to see his kid. But full disclosure, it's not for me to imagine, because that man was me.

There has yet to be any kind of solution offered up for that problem. The average working man, without expendable income, really has nowhere to turn for help offsetting the enormous costs associated with family court legal representation. And this is one reason why America now has what's commonly called "a fatherless crisis." There is a huge number of dads who are being forced out of their homes and families—with the number growing fast every day, and it's due, in no small part, to the inherent bias against men in the family courts. Most states don't even pretend to try to give dads equal rights to their kids in custody proceedings.

Every two or four years, the fatherless crisis provides politicians running for office with a great soundbite. Oh yes, they talk a good talk about the importance of family, but none of them ever does anything about it. And this, all of this, is what led me to *Dad Talk Today*.

The only way to fix the fatherless crisis is to fix the culture. The culture of family used to be a mom and a dad. Now, it's increasingly accepted when a mom isn't just the head of the household, she's also the sole parent in the household. Did you know that in roughly 80 percent of all single-parent homes the lone parent is a woman?[1] Feminism has ruined the nuclear home. But that discussion is a whole other can of worms. Maybe I'll write a book about it someday.

Fixing the culture, man, that's not an easy row to hoe. The best situation for any child, especially in these chaotic times, is that they have both a mother and a father. The only way to get the situation back on track is for good men to take a stand—a stand for families, a stand for achieving a balance in the family court system, which means a stand for dads.

But as you'll see, with a system that's decidedly misandrist, or, in other words, prejudiced against men, taking that stand, and winning, isn't all that easy—like, not at all.

BATTERED AND BEATEN BUT NOT DOWN AND OUT

ONE
THE EMOTIONAL TOLL

I SINCERELY DON'T KNOW HOW a lot of dads make it through every month. I mean, the emotional toll, the money, the fight to stay relevant and involved in the lives of the kids, dealing with a bitter ex—it's just plain exhausting. And it's relentless.

These situations we get into are no-win situations that are torture. Being with a woman who is more interested in hurting you than she is in taking care of your kids is one of the worst things that you could ever go through. Because it's like, if I call the cops, I know what's going to happen. If I leave and try to get out, I'm a deadbeat; I've abandoned the family. It's one of those situations that makes you feel trapped.

Guys, it's a horrible situation. There are dads suffering from extreme depression who don't think there is any way out. I've gone through a divorce, alienation, not being able to afford the family courts, arguments with the ex, financial problems, and having a tough time with the bills. When you're in that dark hole it's hard to get out. It really is.

It's okay to be down, it's okay to be depressed sometimes. What's not okay is to stay there, to stay depressed. If there's a problem, what are we doing to solve it? We cannot allow depression to control us. That's one reason why *Dad Talk Today* exists. Like-minded dads helping each other through the struggles.

Another thing, and this is a point I'll make quite regularly—especially in this book—is that we're fighting a culture war, against the way people look at dads, and false narratives. One of the biggest false narratives is the myth of the deadbeat dad. I've asked on my podcast the rhetorical question for which no one seems to have an answer: "If a mother calls a father who is fighting to be in his kid's life a 'deadbeat,' then what does that make her if she's forcing him to go through an attorney or family court to see the kid?"

A woman once told me in no uncertain terms, "An absent father is a deadbeat, so that makes the mother the protector. An absent father does emotional damage to our babies—more emotional damage than an inconsistent father." Wait a second. She's saying a mother is protecting her kids from the emotional damage created by an absent father, but neglects to mention that the reason the father is absent is because the mother won't let him see the kids! Many of these women block access to the child and then claim the dad is inconsistent. They want it both ways. And sadly, the courts usually side with them.

Let's talk about fathers who are fit, willing, and able. What rights do they have? Well, if you have a good dad, but the mom is a bad mom, she still has more rights to the kids than him. What rights does he have in the family court system? The problem is that state governments make a huge chunk of money off the backs of dads. The courts are designed to profit off them. So, he's going into court likely facing a pre-determined outcome.

I met a guy on TikTok named Robert after one of his videos went viral. Check out what he said. It was an amazing testimony to what men are going through. "I can say with complete certainty that my interaction with the family court system has been significantly more traumatic than war, more traumatic than watching my friends die, and more traumatic than having my body destroyed." Amazing, harsh, yet true and understandable for anyone with personal experience of family court. He continued, "I have the ability to change the outcome of things in any given situation in war. I could try a little harder, I could fight a little harder, I could motivate myself to hold on one moment longer. In this situation, all I could do was stand by and watch the horror unfold while they took everything away from me." There really is a helplessness to being trapped in the family court system.

How can we respond to that? It's not easy. I won't claim it is. But we need a community of men and women armed with information, and a well-considered plan. We may have yet to win the war, but battles are won every day. One day a man named Wayne called into the show excited that after years of fighting in the courts, he won custody of his children. "The kids got old enough to realize she (Mom) was the problem. Now they all live with me… I was losing the fight for a long time. But last month, I finally won." This doesn't happen all the time. But it's one of those small victories—small in the wider view, but huge for Wayne.

Kids are smart. Never underestimate their ability to put the pieces of a puzzle together for themselves. This is a dad who cared, fought, and won.

I want to arm you with the tools to challenge the narrative like Wayne did. Legislators, attorneys, and the system in general have power over you because we haven't successfully challenged the narrative. Oh, but we will.

The best ammo is information. It empowers you against false narratives, gaslighters, lawyers, and ex-wives. I got a call from a guy who lives literally across the street from his children, and he's on the wrong side of an 80/20 custody arrangement. He wanted to know if he had any rights to be able to pop over to see the kids. Guys, you have to know your state laws. In a case like this, that's how you fight.

To a guy, like that guy, who asks, "What rights do I have? Can I do this without the courts?" I say you absolutely can. But there's a rub—the ex has to be willing to do it, too. If she's not, well, you're probably going to have to go through the courts. The thing is, yes, we fight, and we push, and we challenge narratives, but it's okay to engage in civil conversations with your kids' mom. But one of the ways I see in getting the ex to cooperate is to show some vulnerability. Keep your emotions in check. I've said this many times on the podcast, forget the attorney. Forget the formality. Just say, "Hey, we came together, we made a child. We don't want to be together anymore. That's okay. I know we don't always see eye to eye, but if you will name a place and a time, I'll be there. Let's see if we can come together because I want our kid to know that we can do this together." Sometimes that works. Most of the time it doesn't. But if it worked for one dad, then maybe it'll work for you. It's worth a shot.

Here's the sad thing about these conflicts—beyond the toll it takes on dads—is it's the children who pay. And the false narratives? The kids often believe them. But kids have to question things, too. They shouldn't blindly believe the reasons they've been given for their dad not being around. What's unfortunate is they've been programmed to think it's normal when Dad isn't there. So, a kid builds up hatred toward their father because a narrative has been pushed that Dad is just another deadbeat. A lot of kids grow up not having a relationship with a person who would have always been there—had they been allowed. That's the sort of thing killing fathers.

False narratives aren't just words. They're weapons.

Men have it rough. It seems we're not even allowed to hurt—to experience real, heartfelt pain. A dad just wants to be a dad. He doesn't want any of the conflict. All too often guys are navigating pain no one knows about. Then the guy feels like no one cares.

We need to foster conversation. We're brothers helping brothers and you know what? We encourage these conversations. I appreciate fathers because society doesn't. It doesn't value fathers. If you need proof, look no further than some of the man-hatin' pages on social media. I saw a post that read if a baby's DNA doesn't match yours, you still need to man up and take care of that child—that just because it's not yours, it doesn't mean you shouldn't be taking responsibility. Okay, I'm paraphrasing, but my God, lady, what the hell is wrong with you? That's just twisted, perverse logic, and it's aimed squarely at fathers.

But that's what happens. These buffoons even show up on my pages. I've tried to play nice. I tried reducing the amount of "dad talk" in *Dad Talk*. I tried to be more "neutral." You know what it did? Not a damn thing. Actually, it made things worse because it discouraged men from speaking up. The day it really hit me was when we were talking about some of the challenges dads face and some woman slid into the comments whining, "My baby's daddy's this, this, this, this and this." Then a guy jumped in with a reply that has stuck with me to this very day. He said, "Look, you have thousands, literally thousands, of pages where you can go and say the things you just said. This is the one place where I can come to where I feel like I can talk. Will you please just leave us alone?"

Wow! Thank you, sir. That truly set me straight. No more compromise. I love guys like that—the guys speaking up. They're the ones who recognize the real problem—it's not that we talk about dads, it's that we don't talk *enough* about dads. The other side wants to destroy fatherhood—to take out the dad. We need to put the dad back in.

When a dad is being squeezed through the wringer, the pain he feels is often amplified by the feeling that he's all alone—like he has no voice. Hey man, I've been there. It sucks. That's one reason why I started a podcast—to give a voice to the voiceless. There are plenty of dads in this country who feel voiceless. Maybe you're one of them. Buddy, let me say you are absolutely not alone. Tens of thousands of people participate in our *Dad Talk Today* support group—people encountering the same issues as you and with the same stories. We're building a community together, so get in there, lock arms with your brothers, and encourage and empower them to speak out.

But don't be disheartened. If you're going through a tough situation, don't buy into the negativity. Don't attach yourself to the false narratives of the system, or the people hellbent and determined to destroy fatherhood. Don't question yourself—whether you're good enough. You *are* good enough. Push aside the gaslighting. You are perfectly made —special, in fact. Never, ever doubt that.

Men are good. Dads are good.

TWO
DIRTY TRICKS & THE DANGERS OF CUSTODY EXCHANGES

IF DADS DIDN'T have it bad enough facing parental alienation, working for our kids but not being able to see them, paying insane amounts of child support, or facing domestic violence, many also face false allegations. A mom can make a wild and fake claim against the dad, not necessarily because she is crazy, although she may be, but because they work to harm the dad and it will help them win custody and money.

I can't stress enough the pressing importance of these issues. It's one thing to feel as though you're being screwed in a courtroom, in a custody case, but there are dads whose lives are in literal danger. It's not an exaggeration. I've gotten voicemails that are so chilling, they keep me up at night. One guy talked about how his kid's mother was trying to hire a hitman. Can you imagine something like that? A hitman? Why, because he wants to see his kid more than twice a month? Still, I've had other guys say they've had premonitions they were going to be killed at a visitation pickup. They ask me, "What do I do? Should I show up?"

What do I say to that guy?

There is a video titled, "What Are Some Dirty Tricks Used by Lawyers to Win Child Custody Battles," from a lawyer in Utah where he explains how common and effective false accusations are. He explains that one parent can falsely accuse the other parent of being evil, abusing the child, domestic violence, neglect, or drug addiction, with no basis in fact, and it will help them win custody. That's how family court works. He playfully recommends accusing the dad of having a mental illness for success in family court: "Say 'diagnosed,' even if there is no diagnosis, that makes the allegation sound more serious and credible even if it turns out that there is no such diagnosis, it doesn't matter." The lawyer goes on to list other "helpful" false allegations—the other parent's house is dirty, or that they're a criminal or unfit. He advises making claims that you are the only primary caregiver or that the other parent's work schedule can't accommodate joint custody. Then step two is, "Make more such allegations! The more and the scarier, the better. Make enough false allegations and eventually the court will believe some of them."

The way family court is set up, our legal system, alongside the biased support in favor of moms means that these false accusations are highly effective. Yikes. And this is happening every day. The worst part is that the one making the false accusations, even when caught, rarely gets punished. Very rarely.

The dangers for dads are real, and they go beyond false allegations. You've got the dangers at custody exchanges—

men have been murdered in some cases. If an exchange isn't supervised, the mom can accuse you of anything she wants, and, of course, the biased family court system is all too happy to believe her. What's a dad to do? I mean, we can tell them to wear bulletproof vests or to carry a camera at all times. That's not right. No parent should feel threatened when going to pick up or drop off their kids.

We've gotten to a point where dads are saying things like, "I feel like I could die when I go to pick up my kids. Should I go get them?" I can't tell them, "No. Stay home. Don't see your kid." I can't do that. So, what's the answer? Man, I wish I knew. As I've said time and again, I'm not a lawyer. So, until we can change the system, we still have to try to operate effectively within it.

It's not easy. It's not cheap. Some people can fight it—to a point. It's pretty much a losing battle. Admittedly, a few dads have gotten good results inside it, but others were marked the second they stood before the judge.

Family court isn't going anywhere, and the truth is real cases of domestic violence or sexual abuse need to be heard, and that's where they're heard. My take is in cases of simple divorce, you don't need family court. The crux of it is, there are two people who've decided they don't want to be together anymore. Then the lawyers get involved and magnify the conflict—like pouring gasoline on a still smoldering fire—which just complicates everything. That's how they make their money. And that's why family court ain't going anywhere—there's always going to be conflict. Lawyers make sure of it.

The sad fact is dads are in danger. Okay, they're not all being killed—not in the literal sense. But they've been so beat up, beat down, discouraged, and kept from seeing their kids that they feel a part of them has died.

You won't see their stories in the headlines. You won't hear family court judges sharing them in open court. You won't hear about the women telling dads that they'll kill the children before she "allows" them custody. That's called "filicide," or more specifically, "spouse revenge filicide." You won't hear about the dads begging for help—or about the dad living through the consequences of false allegations.

One woman called into the podcast to share the nightmare her husband was living through thanks to a vengeful ex-wife. She recounted how, "His baby mama had him arrested because he tried to make her laugh by lifting her up and dropping her in the snow. They were just joking around, and she called the police." The guy was arrested and jailed for "domestic abuse." So, for the next several years, the husband and the ex-wife were in and out of family court dealing with custody issues, and naturally his arrest sullied the guy before the court. Now, because of those false allegations of abuse and his ensuing arrest, the guy will not attend the custody exchanges with his ex-wife. He sends his mother instead. The guy is terrified, as he should be, and for what? Because a bitter ex-wife tried to destroy his life and used visitation with his kids as a weapon. This dad has suffered through this for ten years. His kids are now young teenagers, so really, who lost in this deal? Who did the mother really hurt? Of course, she hurt the dad, but those kids lost ten years with their father. It's pathetic. At least now the guy has a supportive wife willing to put up with the maniacal behavior of his ex-wife. As she told me during the show, "This is one stepmom who supports your mission and what you're doing and is very pro dad."

How about the guy from San Diego who called into the show to say picking up his kid isn't the problem; it's the drop off when the visit is over. He shared how, "Every time I drop my daughter off I feel like it's the last time I'll ever see her." He's got a manipulative ex and that scares the bejesus out of him. "I feel like the cops are going to be there, I feel like mom is going to manipulate the situation and make it seem like I've done something wrong."

You want to know how to fight against this—how to fight against this system? We've got to change the narrative; we've got to change the culture. I keep saying it. These false allegations piss me off. People are so quick to believe them.

Make sure you're getting both sides of a story because the family court system is a racket. It'll believe every allegation made against a well-meaning dad without looking deeply into whether it's true. This is a theme I harp on relentlessly because it's so damaging. These courts reduce capable and fit dads into mere visitors in the lives of their own children.

There's rarely due process for the guy and it's infuriating.

THREE
GUILTY UNTIL PROVEN INNOCENT

YOU ARE PRESUMED INNOCENT until proven guilty. At least, that's the way it's supposed to be. In theory, that's the cornerstone of the American justice system. In a courtroom, the defendant in a criminal trial is presumed to be innocent, meaning the burden rests on the accuser to prove the guilt of the accused—the accused does not have to prove their innocence. This hallmark of the American legal system is on display in every criminal courtroom each and every day. The one place where you won't see it? The family courtroom. Every father looking for primary or even equal custodial rights in most states has to prove himself worthy. Rarely is a dad *presumed* to be worthy. That distinction typically belongs to the mother regardless of whether she actually is worthy.

Men are walking into family courtrooms and being punished just for being male. One way the anti-dad bias manifests itself is the way men are attacked for mistakes that happened years ago in their youth, as if that somehow determines whether they're a good father. Let's say he used to be a drinker... DENIED. Let's say he lost a job once... DENIED. Let's say he raised his voice once when he shouldn't have... DENIED. In family courtrooms in nearly every state, county, city, and town men are held to account in ways that women simply aren't.

All people are flawed. All people have a past. All people make mistakes. Yet, since the dawn of the family court system, dads asking for custody have always had to prove themselves worthy. They're consistently portrayed as abusers or deadbeats. There's a meme floating around social media that really nails the bias. It reads, "When Daddy's broke, he's a deadbeat, but when Mom's broke, she's doing her best."

Most of the time the skewed perception of dads is pushed by the legal profession. They want the conflict. Conflict is great for business—especially for divorce lawyers, who rake it in. Attorneys will always figure out a way to rig the system.

A dad fighting for a 50/50 custody arrangement will often face an onslaught of unfounded accusations because the mere appearance of impropriety destroys his chances in court. I've seen videos of attorneys telling a client something along the lines of, "You want to win the case? Make sure you get a false allegation in there." It's a despicable tactic, but they do it. What does that say about the attorneys?

Look, I'll agree not every attorney is a shady one. I had a guy comment on my Facebook page, "There should be lawyers that will help dads that can't afford a lawyer." A few of those do exist, and it's a great thought, but the thing is, while there are lawyers who work pro bono, how many do it for dads in custody cases? That lawyer has to eat. That lawyer has a reputation to maintain. At the end of the day, they've got two choices—do what's right or make money.

For a dad, false allegations are nearly impossible to fight. As I said earlier, in this country, dads in family courtrooms don't have the presumption of innocence. They've got to prove themselves and once an allegation is made, it's damn near impossible to change a judge's perception. We've seen it time and again with the #MeToo movement— men destroyed by allegations without any due process to determine whether the allegations are even true. Guys without the resources of someone like Johnny Depp can't afford to fight them, so they end up on the losing side almost every, single time. But even if they win, the damage is done. What then? How do you make that guy whole?

What about a father's reputation? What about the looks and the side-eye glances and the behind-his-back whispers he gets when he picks up his kid from school? There's a group in Idaho called the John Mast Foundation whose sole purpose is to help anyone fighting to be in their kids' lives. It was named for John Mast, my friend, a man who was falsely accused of domestic violence and later exonerated. He spent several years in the courts fighting to see his three kids, and then after winning weekend visitation, he was murdered in the parking lot of a grocery store while picking them up. The guy who shot him—according to police—his ex-wife's father. After his murder, Mast's family and friends vowed to do everything they could to help others going through the same sort of fight Mast suffered through. But what happened in the Mast case is he was hit with false allegations in the beginning, and that gave the mom the upper hand from the very start.

On a related note, one of the comments I received on the podcast that meant a lot to me was from the Mast family. We were working on custody exchanges, trying to figure out what we can do to help out and I asked them, "What is the one thing that you wish that you would have had when John got killed that would have helped you, because I'm trying to find out what we can do?"

They said, "Eric, honestly it was you guys getting on there and doing that show. Because up until then we felt like we were fighting this alone and that no one was listening to us. Then we found this community and that is what helped us through."

Think about that. Never underestimate the power of giving other people a voice.

A person who can make a false allegation that destroys somebody's life and not bat an eye is a sociopath. That's the most apt way to describe them. Any mother who plays that card to win custody of their kid is the real danger to that child because, well, frankly, that child is living with a sociopath. What's the answer to that? How can we protect dads? The only way to prevent baseless allegations against a parent is to beef up the penalties for perjury in family court. You want to stop these vile and evil actions? Throw someone in jail. The minute a false accuser is hauled away to central booking, you can bet dollars to donuts, fewer people will be doing it.

Guys aren't just considered guilty until innocent for false allegations though, they are also considered guilty for mistakes long ago in their past. There was a guy who called into the show who said he and his ex-wife are both recovering alcoholics. He'd been clean two and a half years. She'd been clean three years. He put in a request to change the custody order which had been put in place six years earlier—when their drinking was at its worst—and the ex-wife refused to agree to the change. Obviously they'd both improved their lives. The guy had demonstrable proof for the court that he'd changed but it didn't matter. It's not fair that a dad is expected to be perfect otherwise he can't have custody. Fact is that people are flawed. If a dad has a past with alcohol or drugs, or any issue for that matter, he still has rights as a dad.

Doesn't everybody deserve a second chance?

Oh, and the wife had primary custody. She was an admitted alcoholic, just like the dad. So, why was *she* the primary custody parent in the first place? We talk about equality. Yeah, right. They were both alcoholics. She got more time with the kids than he did—that's why he was asking the court for more. So, where's the equality? There isn't any. He still should still have rights as a father, but he didn't!

These legislators, these attorneys, these judges, they've got no heart. They're not listening. I think, at its core, what we're fighting is the way people look at dads. How can there not be a bias when dads are constantly subjected to false allegations or referred to as deadbeats? It's an exhausting exercise in futility that's so wearing on a dad they are often just too worn out to fight back. As I told a reporter with *Fort Worth Weekly*, "If dads talk about the financial abuse of the system, then they are labeled a deadbeat dad."[1] Why shouldn't a dad be frustrated when most of his money goes to his ex, and he can't even see his own kids? That's the point I hammered home with the reporter —"They are paying somebody who has a new man in the house that moms are getting the kids to call 'Daddy.' The stepdads are seeing their kids more than the biological fathers are."[2] As I will say again and again and again—children and families are not products. Courts shouldn't be putting a price tag on them and charging dads for access. Our rights come from God, not from a court, and they certainly don't come with a price tag.

Dads are regularly having to prove themselves worthy. A guy will be standing there in family court as a judge and the lawyers banter about whether he's a good dad. He's got no presumed rights. There he is having to work to attain even a smattering of respect. How often is the discussion about whether the woman is a good mom? Maybe she has a drinking problem. Maybe she has a drug problem. Maybe she's cheated in the relationship. Maybe she's irresponsible with money. Maybe she has an inconsistent employment history. She still has rights. The default arrangement is that she'll get custody unless by some miracle the dad was able to "earn" his own kid.

Even if you're a great dad, you're going into the game already at a disadvantage. A lot of times, even though you've got all the evidence in the world proving your worth, it doesn't do any good. Many dads who've been fighting the bias and getting nowhere fall into a horrible frame of mind—they begin to believe the lie. They think, "Maybe it's my fault. Maybe I'm not a good enough person." They gaslight themselves. If you're going through this; if you've been the victim of false allegations and parental alienation, you probably feel like you're going crazy. You feel guilty for not being able to see your kids. You wonder if you did everything you could. Then soon enough you're overwhelmed by that guilt.

It's not fair.

But that guy—that guy might be you—and you're thinking how you've been fighting in vain, not getting results, and that the system won't change. You think you're not doing anything; that you should be doing something different. Don't gaslight yourself. Stay in the fight. That's the only way we'll ever make a difference. When did any of us give the government permission to tell us when, where, and how we can see our kids? We didn't. So, let's stop them.

Look, I get it. It's absolutely exhausting fighting this battle. It really is. I'd love nothing more than to jump into a classic Mustang convertible and drive across the country with the top down, wind in my hair, with my only worry being when I'll come across the next Buc-ee's. Who wouldn't want to escape the madness? But ya know what? I can't do that—none of us can, not if we want to make a difference—not if we want to change the biased system and change the narrative. I have to stay in this fight. *We* have to stay in this fight.

If not us, then who?

WHY IS THIS HAPPENING?

FOUR
THE WAR ON MASCULINITY

So, WHAT ARE THE THINGS that skew the perception of dads? To be honest, it's not the easiest question to answer. There are societal biases. There's the imbalance created by lawyers and legislators swayed by money. There's militant feminism. There's the push in mainstream media, from Hollywood to the news, to portray men as villainous, simply because they're men. So, while bias against fathers is difficult to quantify, the end is the same, and it's due in no smart part to two words helping to fuel the animus—"toxic masculinity."

How many times have you heard that phrase? It's everywhere nowadays. For instance, we have a recent WebMD article titled "What Is Toxic Masculinity?" that explains toxic masculinity is "ingrained in some areas of our culture," and we need to "identify it" and "treat it."[1] Or there is this fun article titled, "Are All Men Toxic?" which explains, "Toxic masculinity is a byproduct of patriarchy. The patriarchy is a systematic set of beliefs and customs that centers men in positions of dominance and control. It necessitates gender inequality, as women and other 'minoritized' groups are seen as less than those who have the 'divine' right to rule over others."[2] The prestigious *Atlantic* summed it up best for us: "Over the past several years, toxic masculinity has become a catchall explanation... Many progressives, meanwhile, contend that detoxification of masculinity is an essential pathway to gender equality."[3]

But let's make it perfectly clear—there is no such thing as toxic masculinity. It's a made-up term—one that exists solely to coerce and scare boys and denigrate any man who displays the characteristics of strength. Gender doesn't determine "toxicity." Gender doesn't automatically determine one's behavior. Being born with both an X and Y chromosome doesn't make a person "toxic." And anyone who's honest would admit toxic behavior isn't limited to men. Yet, let's be real, no sensible person would claim a *woman* is inherently toxic based solely on her gender. It's a ridiculous notion from any angle.

When there's widespread denigration of men, of course, it results in bias. It allows a cultural atmosphere where the overarching narrative is, "toxicity resides in all men." How then can a guy walk into a family courtroom and not be at a disadvantage?

Here's the reality—the real problem isn't "toxic" masculinity, it's a *lack* of masculinity. If masculinity is so toxic, then why is the fatherless crisis such an increasingly growing issue? If a kid has no father at home, and the crisis is rooted in that absence, then doesn't it stand to reason that the real problem isn't "toxic" masculinity at all, but rather, the *absence* of masculinity?

Society in general has made masculinity unattractive.

Instead of the old, cool James Bond we now have the aging, struggling James Bond. Instead of Clint Eastwood, Hollywood gives us Michael Scott and Jim Halpert. They pretend the perfect man is the "sensitive" man, but that's a lie, too. Truth is, they revile them as well.

The push to brand strong men as toxic comes in large part from "progressive" advocates, who, lately, have gotten support from the highest level of government. On March 8, 2021, the Biden administration established the White House Gender Policy Council, with its stated goal to "advance gender equity." However, if you read the council's 42-page manifesto titled *National Strategy on Gender Equity and Equality*,[4] you'll see the goal isn't gender equity in any way. It's quite the opposite. Despite the title, the goal isn't equity, you know, leveling the playing field for both women *and* men, it's to essentially elevate women *over* men in every area of life.

It all but admits that the Gender Policy Council is actively working to create a cultural bias that favors women above men...

> Building back better requires not just policy reform, but also *a shift in the social and cultural norms* that undermine gender equity and equality...

And as far at the court systems are concerned? The Gender Policy Council doesn't recognize a problem for men —that the playing field isn't always even. In a section titled, "Promote Gender Equity and Fairness in Justice and Immigration Systems," the manifesto suggests women are the only ones who experience injustice.

> Fair treatment in justice systems and immigration systems is essential to advancing gender equity and equality. However, the unique needs of *women, girls and gender nonconforming people* are frequently overlooked in both systems.

There's not a single word about the "unique needs" of men in the justice systems, or that they're "frequently overlooked."

Another stated goal of the Gender Policy Council is to "eliminate gender-based violence." That's a noble goal, yet there's no mention of the violence experienced by male spouses or male partners, nor is there a mention of a certain CDC (Centers for Disease Control and Prevention) report that shows that the number of male victims of domestic violence is equal to the number of female victims. Evidently, if you believe this bunch, the only people who experience gender-based violence are female.

So, the *National Strategy on Gender Equity and Equality* isn't really about gender equity and equality, is it?

The Gender Policy Council paints women as victims in literally every area of life. It implies the only way a woman can overcome life's challenges is to rely on the government. Truth is, the document is insulting to women, because it suggests there aren't strong, successful women in society crushing it every day, without the government's help, in every area of life. As we know, there definitely are.

If we're not getting honest and objective information from the highest office in America, then how can you expect it anywhere else? How can any man expect to see a change in the family court system if the most powerful person on the planet is himself promoting anti-male bias?

Feminists and "progressives" often toss around the term "toxic masculinity" with such casual ease that it's become white noise. They use the term as a convenience—to simply brand behavior they don't like.

People who put together things like the Gender Policy Council worship the signaling of virtue. Their true aim isn't real gender equity but more the appearance of it. The movement is a religion whose tenets foster the destruction of strong men while devotees stand on the altar of equality. It's a smoke and mirrors morality play where their belligerence and true agenda is masked by virtuous language about how all genders are equal.

Take note of how people like that promote inclusion while fostering divisiveness yet never see themselves as intolerant. And the ones who fancy themselves the smartest in the room can't even tell you how many genders there are.

By the way, the answer is "two."

This is what men face every day in the family court system—biases created by self-indulgent charlatans disguised as caring politicians and pushed by an enthusiastic media filled with activists disguised as journalists, in an age where weak men are lauded, and strong men vilified.

Remember, masculinity is a target for one reason—to destroy the nuclear family and traditional values. Truth is

that the most toxic part of masculinity isn't masculinity—
it's the people who want to abolish it.

FIVE
HOW SOCIETY ATTACKS MEN AND DADS

EVERY SINGLE DAY IN AMERICA there's a dad fighting a battle many people don't understand.

It seems the establishment doesn't want to talk about the challenges men face—the bias in the family courts; the alienation from their children; the accusations of "toxic" masculinity; the scourge of being branded a deadbeat or "less than" simply for being male.

Men are getting screwed six ways to Sunday. Whether it's family court bias, the mental health issues suffered by children because of bad judicial decisions, the fatherless crisis, or the profoundly negative effects of keeping a father away from his children—society turns a blind eye to what's going on.

Why? Part of it is the way society is conditioned. How many times have you heard the phrase, "Happy wife, happy life?" We all have. It's ubiquitous. It's funny. But it's biased. A husband can be happy, too. And you know what? If both the wife *and* the husband are happy, life is going to be happy for *everyone*—especially their kids.

Society's bias against men didn't just happen, though. It's steeped in the deeply rooted ideals of yesteryear; the halcyon days represented in those old black and white television shows. Ozzie went to work. Harriet stayed home with Ricky and David. Ward went to work. June stayed home with Wally and Beaver. Dad's the provider, Mom's the caretaker. It's that old-fashioned, nostalgic vision of a time long gone pushing the thinking of many, many family court judges and friends of the court. A dad walks before the bench, and it's already been decided he should pay support and Mom should have primary custody. On a related note—it's amazing the *Andy Griffith Show* ever got made. It depicts a single dad raising a son on his own.

But men aren't just financial providers; they're also care providers. But, often, the bias, whether subconscious or implicit, makes it impossible for a father to be treated fairly when it comes to custody issues.

Silence doesn't help either. It compounds the problem. When we stand on the sideline, we allow societal bias to ruin families and to threaten the relationships dads should be having with their kids. Look, we must address what's happening in the family courts. It is one of, if not *the*, biggest reasons why so many kids don't have a dad around. These judges, with their predispositions, whether they realize it or not, are ruining families. They're ruining fathers. That means that they're ruining children too. If we don't speak up, then who will? Who will address the real cause of the fatherless crisis? All silence does is allow assumptions about why there's a fatherless crisis in the first place, and what does that do? That allows the narrative of the "deadbeat dad" to prosper. "Well, what did Dad do that the judge denied him custody? Obviously, he's a horrible person and an even worse father!"

I don't care what religion you are. I don't care what race you are. I don't care what gender you are. I don't care what country you live in. Masculinity is being attacked. Fathers are being attacked.

But many people don't realize the same number of men are victims of physical violence by their partners as women. In a survey titled, "The National Intimate Partner and Sexual Violence Survey: 2016/2017 Report on Intimate Partner Violence," the Centers for Disease Control and Prevention (CDC) found that more than two in five men—nearly 50 million—experienced physical violence by an intimate partner, which included being slapped, pushed, or shoved.[1] Many of these men also reported experiencing *severe* physical violence, including being hit with a fist or something hard, being kicked, slammed against something, hurt by hair pulling, or beaten. The CDC found that two in five women reported the same thing—the exact same number as men. So, at the end of the day, the prevailing notion that men make up the bulk of violent, aggressive abusers simply isn't true.

Yet, if you were to survey any random group of people and ask, "Who is most responsible for committing domestic violence, the man or the woman?" you can bet nine times out of ten, the answer will be, "the man." This misconception about men is one reason why many dads are doomed before they ever step one foot inside a family courtroom.

What's worse is the shift in how men are currently viewed by the establishment. There was once a time when a strong man—a protector, a provider—would be lauded. But these days society has so profoundly altered its view of gender that strength in a man isn't celebrated—it's vilified. You've heard it, "Oh, he's toxic!"

A man who works from home is viewed as unambitious, a sluggard, or unmotivated. "Why isn't he at work?" "Why's he going to his kid's little league game?" "Wait, he's walking the dog?!" There's a mentality in some companies that this sort of work/life balance is good for women but not for men. "They're just slackers," they'll say. Interestingly, this issue was addressed by the United States Supreme Court in 1989, when it took up the landmark case, "Price Waterhouse v. Hopkins," but rarely do men benefit from the Court's findings.

Here's what happened. A female senior manager at Price Waterhouse, one of the biggest professional services networks in the world, claimed she was denied a partnership because, for all intents and purposes, she didn't conform to the gender stereotype of a woman. The company, in essence, said she acted too much like a man— she was abrasive, used profanity, was a tough talker—and needed to act more feminine. She sued. The Supreme Court considered the case and ruled that, yes, gender stereotyping is a form of sexual discrimination.

The irony is, here we are, decades later, and clearly many men can make the same claim—they're being discriminated against due to gender stereotyping. Corporate culture often frowns upon men who seek the same sort of work/life accommodations as their female counterparts.

While the "progressive" establishment here in the United States may scream the loudest, the overarching anti-male bias isn't limited to the US. The United Kingdom may have it worse.

In 2011, a man named Tom Martin, who'd been a student at the Gender Institute of the London School of Economics, sued the school and alleged that the course material wasn't only systemically anti-male but that they ignored any research contrary to the narrative that all men are bad, and all women are good. As Martin wrote in an op-ed for *The Guardian*, "You can't deny it. Gender studies is full of male-blaming bias."[2] He argued that the gender orthodoxy ignores the people fighting for equality and challenged institutions of higher learning to help fix the problem instead of exacerbating it: "In a world which verbalizes four times more sexism against men than it does against women, it's high time gender studies set a better example, so we all might emulate it."

Gender bias is hurting men in the workplace, in schools, and, of course, the family courts. A dad named Justin commented on the *Dad Talk Today* Facebook page how he lost visitation with his kids after his wife attacked him, but *he* was the one charged with assault. He wrote, "My ex once hit me with a pot on my head and she got me charged with assault and a bunch of other stuff and played musical protective orders with the kids. I haven't seen them since last Easter, and she took everything from me." The bias against men manifests in real and damaging ways.

So, why isn't society sympathetic to men's issues? Why, if Tom Martin is right, is there four times more sexism aimed at men than women? Why are good fathers—based on gender alone—defaulted to being non-custodial parents with limited visitation? And why doesn't anyone care?

These are questions for which there isn't just one answer. Part of the problem is the relentless onslaught of anti-male rhetoric, much of which comes from the burgeoning wave of militant feminism. Part of it is the result of politicians too cowardly to say anything. They're afraid they'll alienate female voters by appearing unsympathetic to mothers. And a big part of it is too much money lines the pockets of legislators who could make a difference but choose not to.

Judiciary committees are often loaded with family law attorneys—attorneys who make money in a flawed system where if they were to change anything, they'd make less money. The family law industry in the United States is a $50 billion a year enterprise, with special interest groups and lobbyists working hard to make sure it stays that way. And where does that money come from? Fathers and mothers. And where does it go? Lawyers, politicians, and all manner of professional grifters. It's an industry that puts profit over family. They're fleecing American parents and their kids.

Why would any family law attorney serving in a legislature work to change that? It's a gravy train. As with almost any injustice, everything goes back to one mantra—follow the money. Who stands to benefit? Who's getting paid? So, any effort to change legislation will almost always fall upon deaf ears.

Look, it's a bad system, and the virtue signalers of modern society aren't likely to be sympathetic to men's issues... ever. There's no "virtue" in it, and there's certainly no payday. But remember this—there are more of us than there are of them.

So, speak up! Gather! Call for attention! Be glad to be

Dad! Ignore the cynics and the critics, and a change will come.

SIX
HOW DADS ARE ATTACKED IN CULTURE

SOCIETY HAS BECOME INSANELY IDIOTIC in so many ways. Whenever a person notices certain things that are true, obvious even, but unpopular, they get accused of being a tinfoil-hat-wearing conspiracy theorist. Believe me, I know. It frequently happens whenever I talk about the consistently negative portrayals of dads we see in all manner of ways. These rubes just don't seem to understand that just because you don't like my assessment, it doesn't make it untrue.

We know dads are attacked in culture. That's not a conspiratorial statement nor is it made up. It's happening every single day. They're attacked on television, in the school system, in the family courts, and in, well, just about every area of society. When you really begin digging into the issue, and seeing how dads are attacked throughout culture, you'll begin to see things in a completely different way. I certainly did.

Here's an example. I'm a hugely nostalgic person. So, when *Cobra Kai*, the Netflix series reboot of the classic 80's film, *The Karate Kid*, came out, I thought it would awesome. I love that movie! It's what I grew up with it. But as I watched the new series, I realized the inherent problem with it—the way it portrayed dads.

Daniel was without a dad. Johnny had been without a dad, too. Johnny was now a deadbeat, alcoholic father. Miguel had a deadbeat father. Every one of those main characters either had absent fathers or were horrible fathers themselves. Now, if I didn't make it my business to pay attention to dad issues, I never would have noticed this. Dads, pay attention to how you're being portrayed! Sure, somebody will say, "Oh, the producers and writers didn't do that on purpose." Maybe they didn't, maybe they did. Either way, those kinds of portrayals have become the norm, which is unfortunate in that these shows and movies have huge audiences—masses of people seeing dads portrayed in ways that aren't true for the majority of us. Don't think that kind of thing doesn't influence the culture. It does.

They influence how the parenting roles in real life are defined. Let me put it like this—there's an old saying, "You can't build with someone that ain't trying to help you carry the bricks."

We have plumbers. We have construction workers. We have roofers, we have electricians. There are different roles for different people, but they're all working towards the same thing when building that house. And that's what marriage and parenting is supposed to be. It's teamwork. So, you might have different roles. And that's okay. We're not expected to do everything on our own. But if you were to pay attention to most everything coming out of Hollywood, you'd never know the traditional roles of a dad or a mom.

One day on my podcast, I asked people to give examples of good dads in television shows. There was Cliff Huxtable from "The Cosby Show," Tim "The Toolman" Taylor on "Home Improvement," Danny Tanner from "Full House," and Carl Winslow from "Family Matters," among others. A lot of guys chimed in on how it seems that these days, dads are portrayed as deadbeats or bumbling idiots—you know, morons who are accidently blowing up stuff. We saw it more than a few times on "Home Improvement." Or they're lazy or not working, and it's the wife who does everything in the house while the guy just sits around drinking beer.

However, in the grand scheme of things, the issue is way bigger than just the entertainment complex. Dads are attacked everywhere, even within our own schools. I took a deep dive into the education system and, to be honest, I wasn't shocked by what I learned.

I sat down with a group of female students from Clemson University, who told me how the school was, in essence, creating weak men. I asked, "Why do you think that?" They told me their professors are telling them that they literally don't need men—that they don't need help from anybody. What's worse, the women said, is that the professors are doing this in classrooms that include men. The women were incredulous and stated what we all pretty much know by now, "You wonder why there's gender confusion?! Or why men aren't taking those traditional roles anymore?!" They're right. These guys are being told that everything about being a masculine male is wrong, that it's evil, and that women don't want it. But those assertions couldn't be further from the truth.

To help illustrate what we're seeing in the schools, let me return to pop culture for a minute. Back in the 90's, I loved Beavis and Butt-Head, the MTV show about two doofuses whose aimless wandering through life both skewered and memorialized the culture of the decade. The show had been off the air for quite a while, when in 2022 Beavis and Butt-Head returned to the zeitgeist. They were brought back, first in a film called *Beavis and Butt-Head Do the Universe*, and then in a streaming series for Paramount+. So, one day I was on a plane, bored, and saw the new movie pop up on the menu of the inflight channel. I had to watch it. And, wow, there was a scene that was one of the biggest nuggets of gold I'd seen in years.

Beavis and Butt-Head stumble into a college. There on campus they're hearing about white privilege, male privilege, and all manner of societal wokeness. A professor informs Beavis and Butt-Head that they have white privilege. And they're like, what is that? Then the students tell them that they could basically do anything in life without ever getting into trouble or suffering any consequences. Beavis and Butt-Head are told they could get any job they wanted, and that they were literally untouchable. Then the professor looks at them and says she hopes they were enlightened and asked whether their actions would change going forward. Butt-Head responds, "We guarantee it!" The next thing you know, they're busting through the cafeteria doors yelling, "Stand back, we have white privilege!" They proceed to cut in line; stealing food like ravenous wildebeests as Beavis informs horrified onlookers, "We automatically assume we can take what we want, and we don't have to worry about the police." On their way out, Butt-Head informs the confused maintenance man, "This is what we were taught, sir!" Moments later they're stealing goods from the college bookstore and vandalizing the campus, all while claiming, "We're subverting existing paradigms." It would lead to Beavis and Butt-Head stealing and wrecking a police car. Then when confronted by officers, Butt-Head casually informs them, "Eh, sir. Maybe you didn't know, but we have white privilege."

My God, man, it was one of the most blistering pieces of satire I've ever seen.

That scene was hilarious yet sad at the same time because it was so true—that's what they're teaching in our schools. They do the same thing with masculinity—vilifying it. Women are told things like, "You are a victim." "You don't need a man." "A man is going to victimize you." "A man only wants you for one thing." "He has nothing to offer in the relationship." "He is expendable." We've now arrived at a place where we have to push back against those falsehoods. If men in general, and dads in particular, don't then we'll never be seen as equals with women.

Comedian Chris Rock may have shared the best perspective ever during one of his comedy specials. He said, "Only women, children, and dogs are loved unconditionally. A man is only loved under the condition that he provides something. After all, when a man meets someone new, his friends ask, 'What does she look like?' When a woman meets someone new, her friends ask, 'What does he *do*?'"

Nailed it.

Society, and by "society," I'm talking the media, the courts, and the educational system—basically, the entire progressive complex—pushes an agenda that says things like the only reason a woman's not getting child support is because the dad is a "no good" man.

Culture be damned. A dad is way more than a paycheck. Don't ever believe the anti-male propaganda being taught in our universities. Don't ever believe the negative portrayals of dads in film or television are the norm. Don't ever buy into any narrative that uses a wide brush to paint all dads as anything other than loving parents who want time with their kids.

Do think about how dads are attacked in culture. Do realize that we're on the precipice of one of the biggest movements that has ever existed. We've just got to get together and realize the importance of what's happening. So, keep showing up and keep doing what you're doing. Our kids, and all dads, depend on it.

SEVEN
THE FATHERLESS ISSUE

THE UNITED STATES OF AMERICA has a fatherless crisis. In fact, the number of homes without fathers is so enormous that alarms like tornado sirens should be reverberating across every peak and through every valley from sea to shining sea. From school shootings to teen pregnancies, high juvenile crime rates to increased infant mortality, the likelihood of living in poverty to all manner of juvenile behavioral problems—the one common denominator is a home without a dad.

This fatherless crisis is talked about a lot in the media, but they always seem to leave out the family court angle and what's causing the epidemic. Sure, they'll give you the statistics and the awful things that happen as a result, but all they really accomplish is leaving the impression that dads aren't there because they don't want to be in their kid's life. That couldn't be further from the truth. Dads are forced out of their homes.

Homes without fathers cause all manner of societal ills that cannot be fixed unless something is done at the jurisdictional level. It's easy to say but way tough to do, and it won't happen any time soon. There's a reason why the business of divorce generates 50 to 60 billion dollars every year. Why would anyone who profits from it want to change how it works?

The statistics of what happens to kids when there's no dad in the home should scare the bejesus out of, well, most anyone. At last check, one in four children—more than 18 million—live in a home without a father, and that includes biological, step-, and adoptive dads.[1]

And the absence of a father all but guarantees a much more challenging road for any one of those kids as they navigate toward adulthood. A study by the US Department of Health and Human Services found that children living in a home with just a mom, with no father present in their lives, have a poverty rate of 47 percent.[2] That's more than four times the rate for kids in a home with married parents. Think about that. Nearly half of all kids living with just their mom live in poverty. That's not right. No kid should have to live that way.

The research also shows that a child raised in a home without a father present is at greater risk for being abused or neglected; is at higher odds for becoming an alcoholic or drug abuser; has twice the chance of suffering from obesity (which makes them more likely to have heart disease); is twice as likely to become a high school dropout; and a girl is seven times likelier to become pregnant as a teenager.[3] Children also shouldn't have to live in an unsafe home. The ones who live in a home without their biological father are more likely to be mistreated.[4]

Sadly, adolescent boys without a dad at home have

greater odds of engaging in delinquency than the ones who do have a dad at home. When you hear about a crime, look at the parental structure of the one committing it, you'll often find a commonality amongst those criminals—a home without a dad. Children from a fatherless home are at greater risk for behavioral problems, likelier to commit a crime, and at greater risk for ending up in prison.[5] That's not to say all children in homes without dads become delinquents or criminals—not at all. But the data is clear that, statistically speaking, children do have a greater chance for success in life when they're raised in a two-parent home.

Research shows a substantially positive impact on teenagers, boys in particular, when they live with their fathers. Those teens have a reduced risk of dealing drugs and carrying guns, and from falling into all manner of criminal activity.[6]

When a dad is involved in the lives of his children, those children have greater emotional well-being and are generally more socially well-adjusted.[7] They also stand a greater chance of being treated well,[8] and they also do better in school.[9] For children living at home with both biological parents, if their father is actively involved in their lives, that involvement has a profoundly positive effect on academic achievement.[10] So, it's clear how amazing and important dads are. We want to spend time with our kids and when we do, look at the great things that happen.

A study published back in 2017 in the *International Journal of Child, Youth and Family Studies* concluded, "Adolescents in families with both biological parents consistently outperformed their peers, indicating that having a stable family is an important aspect of children's outcomes." The researchers had determined, "…adolescents living with their biological fathers and mothers had the highest GPAs, lowest course failure, and lowest levels of school failure compared to children with stepfathers and nonresident fathers."[11] There really is no substitute for a two-parent, nuclear home in charting a child's path for success. It's too bad that's not really the norm these days, so the importance of dads being in their kids' lives cannot be underestimated.

Now, how did we arrive here? Like most any societal failure, the origin of the failure almost always charts back to government involvement. A couple years ago, I interviewed Jo Jorgensen, a political activist and one-time Libertarian presidential candidate, and asked for her thoughts on the fatherless issue. She told me a big part of the problem is that the government incentivizes the separation of families —just handing out checks to single women with children. Have a kid. Get a check. Jorgensen explained how the "Aid to Families with Dependent Children" (AFDC) program— which began in the 1930's—was being used as a sort of grift by people to get free money.

When it was created, the intent of AFDC was to help a mother who'd lost her husband support her children. She could stay home with her kids. The program, initially rife with good intentions, then shifted into a system to be taken advantage of. According to Jorgensen, that shift picked up steam in the 1980's. She cited interviews with teenage females who expressed a lack of concern for the consequences of getting pregnant because they reckoned, "I'll just go on AFDC and get a check." Instead of working a job, they could have a child, and then the government would give them money. So a government program started to help people who actually needed it, instead financially incentivized single people to have kids, fathered by guys who likely wouldn't be sticking around.

AFDC went a long way in destroying the nuclear family. It not only encouraged single-parent households but favored the ones where the father wasn't in the picture at all. A 2003 book entitled, *Marriage and the Economy: Theory and Evidence from Advanced Industrial Societies*, which was a study of the impact of marriage and labor force participation, put it best, "The AFDC program tended to treat households with a cohabiting male who was not the natural father of the children much more leniently than those with a resident spouse or father of the children. This feature created a clear disincentive for marriage and also a clear incentive for divorce, because women who married face the reduction or loss of their AFDC benefits." [12] See, the government incentivized single parents to stay single, and married parents to become single parents. And who ended up the losers? Their kids, and of course, their dads.

The AFDC would end up being repealed in 1996.

Before we move any further, let me make one thing clear —the biggest mistake we can make as parents is to let the government inside of our marriages and to let them get involved in our home lives. Unfortunately, the government, in many ways, injects itself into nearly every area of our lives—including parenting.

Having a complete nuclear family is the optimal situation, but in America there's a relentless attack on family values. That's really the genesis of this government push to get dads away from their own kids. Dr. Ben Carson, the former secretary of Housing and Urban Development, who grew up in a fatherless home himself, told me in 2021 how a lot of the culture today tries to negate the benefits of the nuclear family and strong family values. "You derive your value system from your family, and if you don't get it from them, you get it from the outside, and frequently what you get from the outside is not conducive to success or to good behavior."

Dr. Carson is right, and that's why we're seeing all of those horrifying statistics of what happens when children grow up in homes without fathers.

None of this is by accident. There's no happenstance to the staggering number of fathers not living with their kids. While a lot of people might not want to believe this, kicking dads out of the home is the goal of many within the government—both federal and state; conservative and liberal.

The shift toward smashing dads really began with the expansion of welfare programs in the 1960's. After the death of President John F. Kennedy, his successor Lyndon B. Johnson launched what was known as the Great Society—a series of legislative initiatives that, among other things, was designed to help end poverty. Yeah, well, like most any problem it tries to solve the government instead made it worse. While some of the Great Society policies included helping the disadvantaged learn skills that would get them into the workforce, it also increased handouts… substantially. By the time LBJ's presidency came to an end, not only did his plan for a wonderful, utopian society die a miserable death, he'd exploded the size of the government and also lost the war on poverty.

So, what does any of this have to do with the fatherless crisis?

Some of those Great Society programs discouraged marriage—as Harvard professor Paul Peterson outlined in *Education Next,*[13] welfare assistance went to mothers only if there was no man living in her home. If she was married to a guy with a job, forget it, she risked being above the income requirement for government help, which meant no check was coming. You now had more people on the government dole, which of course, gives the government greater control of its citizens. And, as I mentioned earlier, it incentivized more single women to get pregnant. The irony is that back in the day, having a kid and getting that government money was one way a woman could gain independence. Sadly though, that resulted in way too many kids growing up in a home without a dad.

The welfare state is a true enemy of the nuclear family.

Seriously, if government programs discourage marriage and *encourage* out-of-wedlock pregnancy, how are they helping anything—other than keeping bureaucrats in power?

In the 1800's, Karl Marx, the author of *The Communist Manifesto,* and then later his uber fan, the head of the former Soviet Union, Vladimir Lenin, knew that one of the most effective ways to gain control of the populace was to attack the pillars upon which America was made strong—the family structure and Judeo-Christian values.

We're seeing it happen before our very eyes—from governmental policies to television to film to music to the emasculation of men and the mainstreaming of deviant educational platforms and behavior.

The good news? We can fix it, but we've got to come forth with a message that resonates with the people. Dr.

Martin Luther King, Jr. did that. He made a difference. As for disenfranchised dads and anyone worried about what the fatherless crisis is doing to our country, we've got to switch tactics. We're trying to get that message out there, but we're doing it wrong. If we weren't, we'd have a greater groundswell of support.

Maybe we need more marching. It worked for MLK. Maybe we need more protesting. Maybe we need more profound action and fewer words.

Legislators only talk about the fatherless issue when it benefits them. Oh, they'll bring it up if there's a school shooting or some such tragedy. They'll exploit the horror of things like that to score political points. "Oh, the kid came from a fatherless home," they'll say. "We need to fix the problem." Then do something about it! Either put up or shut up.

I don't have all the answers, but sometimes the answers for the future lie in the past. Maybe, just maybe, that old Apple advertising slogan is the key: "Think different."

Demand action. Demand accountability. Demand change.

THE PROBLEM IS REAL

EIGHT
WHY ARE DADS DENIED EQUAL PARENTING?

"Equal parenting" should be the default goal of every family court judge.

Period.

Much like the divorce industry, the family court system is also an industry—an extremely profitable one that didn't get that way because dads *aren't* fighting to get into their kids' lives. Collectively, dads have paid billions of dollars in court costs and legal fees and enriched the people invested in keeping alive a wildly flawed and corrupted system. The last time I looked, between 80 and 90 percent of the dads fighting for custody of their children lose. And it's not just the dad who loses, the kids also suffer when dad isn't equally involved in parenting.

Good luck waiting for equal parenting arrangements to be the default in family court. Here's why—the courts don't profit if they *decrease* conflict. They *need* the conflict to profit. The mindset within the system looks something like this: "Let's take these people who once loved each other, who are now engaged in conflict, put them in a courtroom, and amplify the conflict." That's how it works. Day in. Day out.

Look, I'd love to see more couples stay together, to try to work it out, to keep the nuclear home intact. But in the absence of that, I live in the real world, we need to see how the family court system can reduce the conflict. It's amazing I even have to say this, but when parents fight instead of equally parenting, it hurts their kids.

However, you see many different people talking about the fatherless issue but not so much about what's causing it. *Why* do we have a fatherless issue? There's this notion that we have so many fatherless homes because dads don't want anything to do with their children or that they're deadbeats. Again, not true. Divorce court didn't become a multi-billion-dollar industry because of deadbeats who didn't want anything to do with their kids. There are dads fighting tooth and nail to get into their children's lives and they keep coming up on the losing end.

In the family courts, the default setting for any custody issue should be shared parenting—equal for both mom *and* dad. That's what best for the kids. At some point, their needs must be considered.

Texas tried to address the issue in late 2020/early 2021 by introducing and then debating Texas House Bill 803 (HB 803)—legislation that became known as the "equal parenting bill." Its aim was to change the state's unfair standard possession order, which was a default 75/25 arrangement in the event of a divorce. HB 803 called for an equal 50/50 arrangement (if both parents agreed) but allowed the judge the final say. What this meant was even if both parents agreed to equal custody, their agreement could be denied if the judge deemed it wasn't in the child's best interests. Once again, a judge, rather than the parents, would be empowered to decide what's best for their children. So, in essence, even if the legislators passed HB 803, equal custody was *possible* but not guaranteed.

The legislation certainly wasn't perfect, but it was a start.

Quick question: Why are family court judges empowered to be the sole arbiters of what's best for dads, moms, and their kids? In criminal courts there's a reason why a jury of peers decides the outcome of a case, yet in family court, a judge decides. There's something inherently wrong with granting someone that kind of life-altering power.

HB 803 was sponsored by 22 state representatives, and for those keeping score, it included 16 Republicans and six Democrats. For the most part, there was zero opposition to the bill. It crossed party lines and in public hearings debating the merits of HB 803, legislators heard from scores of people expressing support for it. You know who *didn't* support the measure? The Texas Family Law Foundation—a lobbyist group for lawyers known for fighting against equal parenting bills. Well, of course they would oppose HB 803! As we've made clear, lawyers make a whole lot more money when parents engage in legal conflict and custody fights.

Few things demonstrate how the bought and paid for family law community views equal parenting than what happened at a rally of HB 803 supporters outside the capitol in Austin. There on the steps, about 200 people gathered to express their support. Just ten people showed up to oppose it. Want to guess who those people were? People who sided with the Texas Family Law Foundation.

Despite huge support across Texas from people on all sides of the political spectrum, HB 803 is dead. The legislation was left pending in committee and never did receive a hearing in the Juvenile Justice and Family Issues Committee —a committee chaired by Democratic Representative Victoria Neave of Dallas. She's a lawyer whose third biggest campaign contributor in 2022 was the political action committee of the Texas Trial Lawyers Association—yet another group that benefits when parents end up in court.[1] As I have said time and again—when there's no conflict, there's no need for court, which means no massive fees for lawyers financially incentivized to keep the conflict going. And we wonder why the state legislatures aren't helping.

Texas isn't alone in claiming it cares about equal parenting and then doing nothing about it. Florida is right there with them. What is it with states like this where on the one hand they'll push an equal parenting bill, and then on the other, allow lawyers to destroy it? Actually, we know the answer. Money. Unscrupulous lawyers profit from parental misery, and they damn sure don't care about your kids. As Matt Gaetz, the United States representative for Florida's First Congressional District told me, "There are people who get rich based on the divisions created within families and based on the desire to litigate rather than resolve things in the best interests of children."

The Florida Legislature passed Senate Bill 668 in 2016, which, instead of granting one parent sole custody, would make equal parenting the norm rather than the exception. As in Texas, there wasn't a whole lot of opposition to it, but also as in Texas, the opposition it did get came from lawyers. The loudest voice railing against it was the Family Law Section of the Florida Bar. Of course. That was to be expected. But, despite their opposition, they aren't the ones who ultimately derailed the bill—it was Republican governor, Rick Scott.

Scott, who is now a United States senator, vetoed Senate Bill 668. In dismissing it, he wrote that he thought the bill would jeopardize the needs and interests of children, "in favor of putting the wants of a parent before the child's best interests by creating a premise of equal time-sharing."

But it didn't end there. Scott would veto a shared parenting bill not once, but twice. He did it again in 2018. Gaetz sums it best: "It's another issue where the special interests have overcome common sense."

You have to give the parental rights advocates in Florida their props, though. They refused to stop pushing a subsequent shared parenting bill—Senate Bill 1796 (SB 1796) which in essence, would have made shared custody the default in divorce cases. The provision read, "The court shall order that the parental responsibility for a minor child be shared by both parents unless the court finds that shared parental responsibility would be detrimental to the child." In 2022, SB 1796 came across the desk of Scott's successor, Governor Ron DeSantis.

He vetoed it.

DeSantis's explanation for why he killed SB 1796 was that he thought it was unconstitutional under Florida law. He worried it could be applied retroactively to already existing divorce settlements. "If CS/CS/SB 1796 were to become law and be given retroactive effect as the Legislature intends," DeSantis wrote in his veto letter, "it would unconstitutionally impair vested rights under certain preexisting marital settlement agreements."

You know whose views DeSantis sided with? The Family Law Section of the Florida Bar—yep, the loudest opponents of SB 1796. Lawyers.

DeSantis's excuse was a cop-out. He's lawyer himself and so, of course, he sided with lawyers. He knows shared parenting hurts the bottom line for the profession and ultimately hurts the coffers of the state's family court system.

Among the SB 1796's biggest critics was former state representative Emily Slosberg-King, a Democrat from Palm Beach. Her occupation? Family law attorney. Naturally. At the time, Slosberg-King claimed the presumption of shared parental responsibility would create "a procedural legal hurdle for self-represented litigants to overcome." Oh, so it would hurt someone *without* a lawyer? Undoubtedly that's what a lawyer would say.

What many of the people pushing for SB 1796's believed was that the presumption would create an equal playing field for both parents in the family court. Again, and this is a theme pervasive in the issue, the people who profit from parental conflict will never agree to reform.

And as usual, besides the dads getting screwed, it's the children who suffer. A study published in the *Journal of Family Psychology* showed that children of divorce fare much, much better when there's a joint custody arrangement. Dr. Robert Bauserman, who, at the time was with the Baltimore Department of Health and Mental Hygiene, looked at nearly three dozen cases that involved more than 2600 children. After digging into the case data of roughly

1800 kids living in a sole custody household, and more than 800 kids in joint-custody arrangements, he determined the results showed, "children in joint custody are better adjusted, across multiple types of measures, than children in sole (primarily maternal) custody."[2]So, there is no reason, none, to prevent shared parenting legislation. It's good for the kids. But even so, you have to wonder whether shared parenting legislation would be the game-changer we'd like it to be. It could just be but one drop in a vast ocean of inequity. I don't know, I'm not a lawyer, politician, or sooth-sayer. I will say as long as a bias exists against dads—where what they say is dismissed or devalued—why would I believe a shared parenting bill would make anyone within the system give a damn about what any of us have to say?

It's moot anyway. Most states don't have any sort of shared parenting legislation. You can count on two hands how many do. It's emblematic of the power of the law lobby. Not unlike the mafia, it does all it can to protect its financial interests, even if it destroys children and their dads in the process.

NINE
HOW THE CHILD SUPPORT SYSTEM IS BROKEN

THERE'S A REASON WHY the courts and so many mothers want to deny a dad his equal rights—the money. It's all about money. Child support is one of the main reasons the system is the way it is.

It's always about the money.

Dad has to carry the primary financial burden of child support, which doesn't just benefit the mother, it's also a huge score for the state. States receive federal incentive payments to collect child support. The more money mom gets from child support, welfare, or other programs, the bigger a cut the state gets. Here's how that grift works—if a parent applies for state assistance, then that parent grants the state the right to keep a share of the child support for as long as the parent is collecting benefits. Once the state gets its share of the child support collections, it sends another share over to the federal government.[1]

God help you if you're a non-custodial dad living in California—the state makes millions of dollars by keeping a disproportionately high share of child support collections.

The national state average is just under four percent. California keeps more than three times that—a whopping 14 percent.[2]

I had a few guys from California call in who described just exactly how their exes personify the system there. Eric said, "I was in a seven-year custody battle with my ex. As soon as we went to court, she quit her job. She went on welfare and purposely made me pay child support." Then there was this guy whose ex did the same thing, only then made him pay for *another* guy's kid. "So, we were doing pretty decent but just because we went to a family court, she left her job right away. I don't mind paying for my own kids, but it is a problem when I have to pay for her, and her lifestyle, plus she got knocked up by her coworker while she was with me. She was cheating on me with her coworker who became her husband... so, when I spend for my kids, I know 100 percent that it doesn't go to my kids, it goes to her other two kids with her new husband." Why is he having to pay child support to a person that doesn't work a job? Why is he having to pay to support kids that aren't his? His wife has an affair, gets pregnant, quits her job, and remarries but the court just automatically says, "She's getting custody, now pay up!"

Money is the root. It always is. Why do you think the injustices in family courts aren't ever seriously dealt with? Why do you think state legislatures aren't changing anything? My God, child support is a cash cow! Why would they change one, single thing? States make millions off the backs of dads, many of whom are drowning in debt trying to keep up with exorbitantly high payments. Children are surviving on less because states keep a portion of their money. What an absolutely shell game the government is running.

Like you, I'm a regular guy, and certainly not the perfect dad. But what I am is this—a guy who never even had the chance to go through the system because I couldn't afford the attorneys. I felt hopeless and, worse, I felt ignored. Nobody listened to me. Nobody listened to the struggles of a dad fighting for his kids. It didn't take long before I realized that if you want a voice in the family court system, you're going to pay for it—six ways to Sunday. You're going to pay for the attorney. You're going to pay the child support. You're going to pay the alimony. And even after you've paid all that money, you're still no closer to having the same rights to your children as their mother.

The child support system is a crap system fueled by the almighty dollar. In the end, the only people who really benefit are the lawyers. And if you fight against it, you're branded an angry deadbeat who doesn't want to pay child support. The system is entrenched in an archaic mindset—a system that does nothing but profit from your pain. So, do we work within that system? Do we work outside of it?

See the challenge?

I could have stayed that guy, but I woke up and said, "No! You are not going to profit from what I'm going through! You are not profiting from my family's pain!" The family courts and the family law lawyers don't see things the way the regular working dad sees them. They don't see that the money I'm paying them comes from the overtime I have to work to afford it—time that I could be spending with my kids. Then they'll turn around and say, "Your Honor, he's inattentive to his children. He doesn't spend enough time with them." It's a vicious cycle, where to afford a lawyer to help you fight for your kids, you sacrifice time with your kids so you can work to earn the money, only to later be told, you don't have rights to your kids because you don't spend enough time with them. It's the exact same thing with overly high child support payments.

How completely jacked up is that?

As if that wasn't enough, when some mothers take the child support checks they use it more for themselves than for their child.

God help you if you should fall behind on a payment. Maybe you suffered a work injury; maybe you were laid off, downsized, or had your hours reduced; maybe an unexpected expense arose… the courts won't revise the amount of your payments. Well, that's not entirely true—once in a blue moon they will. You can submit a request for relief every three years or so in most states, but not only is it rarely granted, a lot of times a dad will be ordered to pay *more*.

Maybe you're a salesman and you had a great year. The amount of ordered support will likely reflect that. But what if the following year isn't as profitable? One time we got a caller into our show, Bob, who had a one-time extra bonus of $85,000 and then the courts based alimony and child support on that, even though he used company documents to prove it was a one-time bonus. Afterwards, Bob said, "I would get my regular paycheck, and 60 percent of it would automatically be gone for income reduction order. Then after tax, health insurance, repayment of a 401k loan to buy a property that was taken away from me in the divorce, I still had to continue paying that. After all those deductions, I was left with just $25."

Can you imagine that? Working hard, working a good job, then government comes in and takes all your money for child support until you're left with literally $25? That just wrong.

What's worse is Bob had to pay attorney fees for his ex-wife, and his ex-wife's attorney was making campaign donations to the judge who handled this case in family court. This is criminal. It's extortion. It blows my mind that this circus just keeps on going.

A lot of times what they'll do in family court is they'll come in, look at a man's W2 forms for the last five years, and either take the average, or the highest year, and base everything on those numbers. But what happens if a few years ago you were crushing it at work but then things took a bad turn?

This gets back to the money the government makes on dads' pain. They do that with the appalling Title IV-D program, a federal law requiring every state have a child support enforcement program. The federal government funds this program, so it gets involved, which means everything becomes about the money rather than what's best for dads and kids.

The way this system got started is you go back to federal welfare programs. Many decades ago, the federal government was looking at situations where there was a kid with a mom who didn't have any money, and she would go on welfare. The government was paying out the cash to the moms but wanted to get it back. So, it had the state governments go after dads to recoup that money. In the late 1990's, child support cases in the US were put under the Title IV-D program, and for every dollar spent on enforcement the state was reimbursed 66 cents. So, what this means for today is that the federal government incentivizes the state to hire more people to collect child support, which in turn incentivizes them to create more situations where child support has to be collected. It's what they do to justify their job and line the state's bank accounts.

Overly aggressive child support calculations result in leaving a dad, not just without money, but without much time to spend with his child... because he's trying to earn more money just to eat. Does that sound like a deadbeat dad who isn't trying?

The thing is, this system and the flow of money seem to run in only one direction—from the dad to the mom, and rarely the other way around. The rules never seem to be as rigid with moms as they are with dads. I had a dad call in to the podcast who told me that he was the custodial parent and his child's mom was ordered to pay child support, but she had yet to pay one red cent and yet nothing happened to her. Stories like that are not uncommon. I hear them almost every single day. Why are deadbeat mothers not held accountable? Shouldn't the law be the law? They'll talk endlessly about equality, but in today's world, men are considered anything but equal.

Oh, one side note about that guy—even though his child's mother never paid the court-ordered child support, he never once prohibited her from seeing their child. Not once. How often do you hear of a mom doing the same thing?

I'll be blunt—it sucks. Most dads give and give and

give, and often receive little appreciation relative to what they're providing. Every day a dad wakes up and works a job he probably hates so he can financially support his kids, only to be taken advantage of by a mother who either, a) doesn't use the support money for the child, or b) demands more money. What's particularly galling are those instances when a mother moves on and into another relationship and uses the child support checks as income more for herself than for her child. Then you've got a dad writing checks that are, in essence, supporting someone else's lifestyle.

For every dad who has fallen victim to this system, there's a mother who loves it. Imagine having gone through a divorce and your ex has enough money that you could live off of their support checks for as long as you remained single. You'd never remarry. Factor kids into that, and you'd never have to work another day... well, at least until the kids turned 18. That's a helluva deal, wouldn't you say?

That's why so many people love the system just the way it is.

You go through this system, where they say, "Show me you're a good father." And when you're done jumping through the hoops, they'll hit you with, "Here's the bill. Now pay up." These people must feel pretty good thinking dads have to prove themselves worthy of what is already their God-given right. The fact that these decidedly not-impartial courts exist in the first place, is a farce.

It's easy for a greedy or retaliatory mother, with support from a corrupt family court system, to say, "Oh, he's a bitter guy who doesn't want to pay child support." That too is crap.

I've been the guy on the other end of a false and frivolous claim. I've paid my child support only to be told I couldn't see my kid. Guys, I understand your anger. I understand your frustration. I've been in your shoes. I will say this unequivocally—I'll be damned if I'm going to pay child support and not be able to see my child. Fight for your rights. The system isn't going to suddenly become altruistic and start caring. It'll play mind games by asking, "Don't you believe your child needs to be supported?" The system will always speak up when the money isn't flowing. Remember, the money is all it really cares about.

Sure, a parent needs money to provide for the child. But it's the politicization of child support that's the real issue. And, the system, that is to say the lawyers, offers up another challenge dads contend with daily—systemic gaslighting. "Hey, it seems like you haven't seen the kids in a while," they'll say as you work two jobs to cover the child support. They want to shame you—to convince you that you're crazy for thinking the system is one-sided, and to guilt you into believing you're some sort of deadbeat. If there's an issue it becomes, "Ya know what? Maybe you just shouldn't see the kids at all. We're going to get a third party to come and sit down with you and the kids. Oh, yeah, you're going to have to pay for it." Guess what? If you love your kids, you'll pay for it. It's criminal.

In this system, you're almost always presumed guilty until proven innocent. Although innocence doesn't even seem to matter a lot of times.

My kids don't have a price tag. Any name you want to ascribe to me, go ahead. Think that'll keep me from speaking up? From fighting back? Good luck with that. It won't. You and I have to be the difference makers. Politicians? Forget it. If they were real leaders, they'd be talking about this. They'd be doing something about it. Churches? If they truly cared about stemming the fatherless crisis and wanted to see things get better, they'd be talking about this. They don't. So many people just do not want to talk about the issues. Is it comfortable to talk about? No, not really. But here's what I'll say to you—disturb the comfortable.

There is power in numbers. Dads unite. A fully committed movement cannot be silenced. Oh, they'll try. Cancel culture is going to come after us, but it won't win. The naysayers in any movement, you know, the complacent and the comfortable believe, "Oh, you can't reinvent the wheel." Hell yes you can! Collectively, we can change the system. We need to stop pussyfooting around and start screaming like we're in the old 1980's hair metal band, Twisted Sister, "We're not going to take it!"

Like any issue, though, to fix it, you must get to the root of the problem. These support issues really begin with the divorce. The essence of the problem is male/female conflict. Marital problems? Co-parenting problems? They're not going anywhere. They're about as certain as anything can be in an increasingly uncertain world. Yet, the system has never really quelled the desire for either person in the conflict to destroy the other for their own gain. No one goes into divorce court to pay compliments to the other person. Most of the aggrieved want the exact opposite—scorched earth. The saddest part is you made a child with them. You've been as intimate as one can be with another human being. You built trust, you shared vulnerable moments, you loved each other. Then, as the pain, anguish, and anger of the breakup kicks in, you find yourself in court hurling insults like baseballs. "She did this." "He did that."

Interestingly, in the family court, the judge and the lawyers do the exact same thing. They also throw those hardballs. You'd better have your mitt ready, too. "I'm not that guy!" "I'm a good dad. I'm a great dad!" The court actually amps up the conflict. It's the perfect system, really —for them, anyway. It bases everything on conflict because the conflict creates cash.

As I've written repeatedly, in this system, cash is every-thing. I can't count the number of dads who were awarded joint custody yet the amount of child support they're ordered to pay is the same as it would be if they only had the kids every other weekend. Talk about an unfair financial burden—not only does he cover the cost of his child's support at his own home, but he's paying for the mother's share, too. The mother has no financial obligation whatso-ever, even though it's a 50/50 arrangement. Still think the family court system isn't biased against dads? You'd better rethink that one.

As long as the bias exist, it feels as though we fight a losing battle. But I promise, if we keep at it, this movement will break the bias, bust the narrative, and neutralize the stigma.

Because at the end of the day, kids need a parent not a paycheck.

TEN
EVERY OTHER WEEKEND ISN'T ENOUGH

IF YOU'RE A NON-CUSTODIAL DAD whose visitation schedule consists of every other weekend or twice a month, you know the disconnect when you first see your kid. Two weeks seems like a month and a lot can happen in a very short period. The weeks goes by, the kid shows up—or you pick them up—and it feels like you're meeting for the first time. You're relearning what they like, what they've been doing, and they have to reacquaint themselves with your house rules. But by the time they get comfortable with all of that, the two-day visit ends and they're headed back to Mom's. Then it's "rinse and repeat"—basically what I call the cycle that doesn't end until they turn 18. And if you think this doesn't hurt your kids, you're wrong. And that's not just my opinion—it's science.

Researchers call it "Attachment Theory," which was developed in the late 1960's through to the late 1980's by the well-respected psychologist and psychoanalyst, Dr. John Bowlby. He determined that children—especially young children—need to forge a bond with their caregivers, which, I would argue includes both the mother and father. That bond greatly influences a child as they grow into adulthood. Bowlby found that a parent's attachment plays a hugely important role in terms of their child's emotional, mental, and social development. So, when we talk about an "every other weekend" visitation schedule, the child's attachment is disrupted. Their development is disrupted. It's devastating for them. So, any family court judge who says, "I have to consider what's in the child's best interest," only to turn around and approve every other weekend visitation is a liar. They don't give a damn about what's best for the child.

I remember a comment from a mom posted on my Facebook page that perfectly illustrates the attachment theory. She mentioned how her daughter, after one particular weekend visit at her dad's, came home and displayed a certain level of detachment. She recounted how the kid was disengaged for two solid weeks before slowly morphing back into her old self. The mom admitted that she didn't handle it well at first but that over time the situation leveled off. The mom described how there was a wide difference between what her daughter experienced at her dad's versus what she experienced with her. There were two different sets of rules. Then of course, the poor kid has to try to adjust. It can't be easy for any kid.

Nevertheless, the system, that is to say the family lawyers and their so-called expert therapists, whitewash the impact detachment has on these children. They'll call it "the suitcase life." Ha ha ha. Isn't that cute?

You know, it's not funny. The detachment is real, and it hurts kids. While the cogs in the wheel admit the constant moving back and forth damages children—that they can't get adjusted and don't feel settled—they still never openly support a default 50/50 custody arrangement. One of the arguments you will hear in court is, "Well, they're in school, so the child needs to stay with the one parent to avoid disruption." That too is a bogus argument. If you applied that reasoning to every case then every parent who's ever had to relocate for a job should lose their kid—ya know, because they were uprooted and moved to a different town.

What's especially galling is how they'll use the alternate weekend visitation order as an excuse for the fatherless crisis. The definition of a fatherless child is a child who resides in a home without a biological father. So, when you have an alternate weekend visitation schedule, technically speaking, that makes the child fatherless. Still, the anti-dad advocates will grasp at any straw to shut down the benefits of equality and a 50/50 custody arrangement.

Attachment Theory really is more than just a theory. We've seen the importance of a child's equal interaction with both parents. The entire issue cannot, and should not, be downplayed. The attachment system is more important than nutrition. The attachment system is more important than homelessness. The family court system must implement a default 50/50 custody arrangement because a child needs unfettered access to both their parents.

We did a show on Father's Day and man, was that a hard day. We opened the day up for comments and there were so many hurting dads sharing similar stories. "There is no worse feeling ever! I dread this day," one guy said, and he wasn't alone. That's what it's like on Father's Day when your kids are kept from you. It should be a day of celebration. Another dad said, "It's devastating! I love you kids and have never given up. I never will! I've never wanted to be anything but a great father! And I'm still swinging the bat. I'll never quit!" Good for you, man. Never quit.

Another father said, "My three girls are obstructed from calling Grandpa, uncles, cousins, and Dad today because the other parent is so scared of the love and bond between all of them! We all still love you girls and are still here when you get out of prison in your own home." See, that's the side of the issue few people talk about. When a dad is alienated from his kids, more often by a vengeful mom, it hurts more than just him—it hurts aunts, uncles, grandparents, and siblings. There are so many people who want to give love and who want that relationship, who are denied. It's evil.

It doesn't help when politicians tout laws they pretend are good for dads, when they are, in reality, hurting dads. In 2022, Governor Ron DeSantis signed House Bill 7065 (HB 7065) which allots $70 million to organizations to promote fatherhood in Florida. The bill's primary aim is to encourage dads to take an active role in the lives of their children. Advocates will say that the bill promotes fatherhood by helping to fund programs and policies to help dads—that they alleviate the barriers dads encounter when trying to be involved in their child's lives. Again, I say, that's BS.

What will HB 7065 do for fatherhood? Not what they tell you it will. No. Instead, it'll ultimately force dads in Florida to pay more child support. It also doesn't address the fatherless issue—not like it's been sold. It also doesn't address the problems with the family courts. All it says is, "Oh, man, we need to get you guys some better jobs so you can make more money." Guess what happens when you make more money? More money goes back to them—the state, the lawyers, and the family court system. This is the kind of phony legislation disguised to look like it's for you guys, but it's really for them. It feeds back into the system. This is all smoke and mirrors. It does nothing good for fatherhood. This is a law designed to make more money off the backs of fathers.

As Brooks McKenzie, my frequent podcast guest from Texas who holds a PhD from Texas Christian University says, "The greatest promoter of fatherlessness in Texas is our family court system." Which, of course, includes judges and the family law attorneys. But, trust me, Texas isn't the only state guilty of this. However, there are states that, at least on the surface, appear to be making some headway.

As I write this, the latest effort to require a 50/50 custody arrangement is pushing forward in Ohio. House Bill 14 (HB 14) would change state law to make an equally split arrangement the default order in custody cases. Any argument to alter that split would require the case be proved with "clear and convincing" evidence. That's a higher bar in the legal sense than what's typical in custody cases. Sounds pretty good, doesn't it? Yeah, well, not to everyone. Take a guess who opposes HB 14—the legal profession: prosecutors, lawyers, judges, you know, all of the people who stand to lose the most if the bill is signed into law. These people think they know what's best for your kids. They look down on you and your ability to make sound parental decisions. They're despicable. In early March 2023, Ohio state representative Rodney Creech told the state's House Families and Aging Committee, "Ohioans don't trust the courts, and it's our duty in the legislature to keep the courts accountable." So, now you know another reason why the judicial system is opposed to the HB 14.

Over in Georgia, House Bill 96 (HB 96), introduced in 2019, would also do what the Ohio bill is attempting to do —create the legal presumption that a 50/50 shared parenting arrangement is in the best interests of the child. It would also compel any judge who rules differently to specifically explain in their order why it wouldn't be in the child's best interests. Oh, look at that—accountability. You don't see that every day in the family court system. HB 96 just kind of fizzled the year it was introduced but was revived in 2023. When this book went to press, the bill was being redrafted and possibly making its way back to the Georgia house.

Kentucky passed a shared parenting bill in 2018 which created the presumption that joint custody and equally shared parenting time is in the best interest of the child. The state is still screwing dads when it comes to child support issues, but at least dads won the shared custody battle. See, there's something to be said for dads who refuse to quit fighting for their rights and the rights of their children.

Never. Ever. Stop. Fighting.

People who refused to quit are why West Virginia now has a 50/50 shared parenting law. The "Best Interests of

Child Protection Act" went into effect in 2022 and the state congressmen who pushed the bill to victory in the senate credited the grassroots efforts of people who felt cheated by the system.[1] As usual, it was the lawyers and the lobbyists who fought against the bill. But the resolve and the fervency of dads fighting the system cannot be overestimated.

While we can be encouraged by the victories and the gains, there is still a very long way to go.

Dads in Texas are certainly fighting. And they don't fall for the smoke and mirrors the state shovels like manure in the stockyards. Texas came out with an expanded standard visitation schedule. But lawyers are skilled in sleight of hand tricks—or more aptly described, "funny math." They'll tell their client—a dad—"Oh, well, you actually get *more* time on certain years." They'll show them a little chart, and the dad's like, "Oh my gosh, it's more than 50/50!" It's total gaslighting. Let's say the dad gets his kid on a Friday night at 11:59 p.m., the lawyer counts Friday as an entire day. If Dad then drops the kid off 6:00 a.m. Monday, they'll count Monday as a full day. So, any minute a dad has during the day, these despicable lawyers will count as a full day—that's how they sell it as, "You've got *extra* days!" Can you imagine trying to pull that with your ex's lawyer? "I think Jane should have this custody arrangement. It's more than 50/50!" You know how that will end—in a hail of four-letter words.

Smoke and mirrors. That's all it is. These politicians have no qualms about giving you guys 50/50 parenting time, as long as it doesn't affect their wallets. At the end of the day, that's all that matters to them—not "the best interests of the child." But still I say, do not be discouraged. Victory is there for the taking. We've seen battles won! Dads are winning in a lot of places. So, stay the course. Band together. Roll up your sleeves and do the work. Stay educated on the issues. Organize yourselves. Be relentless in getting into the ear of your representatives.

WHAT'S A DAD TO DO?

ELEVEN

WHERE DO HURTING DADS GO?

HURTING DADS. WHERE CAN THEY GO? This is a question that I hear literally every day. For one, I certainly hope they come to my podcast. I'm here to lend a sympathetic ear and to rally and work with other dads to change the family court system. The time is right here, right now. I don't care what religion you are. I don't care what race you are. Masculinity is being attacked. Fathers are being attacked, and the point of this entire enterprise is to get the message out there, anywhere and everywhere. *Dad Talk Today* exists to fight for father's rights—to change the narrative about dads, and to offer some sort of respite from the crap you wade through daily.

As I've said, a few years ago I was that guy. I was that guy sitting in that empty house that once had my family in it—the house I came home to every night. Then one day I found out there's another man in the picture and the next thing you know, I'm going through a divorce. I didn't have the money to go through that, at least not successfully. To lose my family, which is the single most important thing in my life, just crushed me. It broke my spirit. It crushed my pride, which kept me from telling anyone what I was going through. To be cheated on—that was humiliating. The last thing I wanted to do was tell anyone, heck, I wanted to hide. I sure didn't want my kids to know about it. And as much as I was hurting, I knew my kids were hurting. So, I put on a mask. That's what a lot of guys do just to make it through the day, to keep them sane, and to stay the course in the fight for the kids.

But what happens to the guy who doesn't wear that mask? They get home, they're all alone in that bed where their spouse used to be. They're all alone on that couch where their family used to be. They've got no one with whom they can share their problems. And the loneliness is sometimes amplified by a woman deliberately trying to isolate you from friends and family. It happens more often than you might realize.

Before he was murdered, John Mast came on my show to talk about the problems he was going through. He had one of the most beautiful families I've ever met in my life, the most humble and supportive people around. They were there for John every step of the way, whether financially or emotionally, coming to court to fight for custody, and even on the day he died they drove four hours for that custody exchange to be there for him. But John told us that when he was in a relationship his ex was putting a wedge between him and his family—just trying to isolate him from them.

If you've got someone who is trying to take you away from your family, your friends, your coworkers, that's a big red flag.

Guys, you need to form a group and you need to start

building each other up. You need to help each other emotionally, mentally, and legally. A lot of dads are suffering through trying times with nowhere to turn. That's one reason why *Dad Talk Today* exists—to give you a place where you know you'll find a sympathetic ear, a safe place to talk.

There's that lonely dad, maybe he's got no money and has lost hope. There's that dad consumed with the nightmare thought he won't get to see his kids. There's the dad who thinks he has nothing left to give. But there, among these dads, is the answer to all of this. A group of men, with the same common concerns, who, collectively, can change everything. There's a Bible verse, Ecclesiastes 4:9-13, that sums it up best—"Two are better than one, because they have good return for their labor; If either of them falls down, one can help the other up." Be that guy who helps the other up. Be that guy who leans on the other to help you up.

Despite what some might say, men aren't afraid to express their emotions, they're afraid of their emotions being used against them. Let's say for example a dad is getting hit with heavy child support, how could talking about that be used against him? Well, some people will say, "Yeah, you're nothing but an angry deadbeat who doesn't want to pay child support." That happens.

One day not too long ago, a guy called in to *Dad Talk Today* and said, "Good morning, Eric. Thank you for all the work you do, from all the dads in Iowa. This show is officially a part of my therapy. It means a lot that I'm not the only one speaking up on the BS against men." Man, it was just kind of a normal comment, but it really meant so much to me, and it shows the importance of getting these spaces for men. Shortly after that call, we got response to it from another dad: "You do not stand alone, brother!" I love it. This is exactly the type of support we need.

You know there is this saying, "Hurt people hurt people." If that's true, why aren't we trying to reach out to those hurting people and say, "Hey man, I'm hurting too, but we can heal together."

Maybe you did some regrettable things in the past, so what? You're a good dad. You don't deserve to go through a system that hates you. We need you—you are important. You do matter! Get involved in the fight! Where do you hurting guys go? Come here and speak up. Shout from the rooftops and tell the other dads what's going on. So many dads are isolated and alone. They need you.

One of the biggest issues that affects dads, to the point where they are so ashamed that they won't ask for help, is domestic violence. Some dads are victims—more than you might realize—and many suffer in silence. They're embarrassed and they think, "Who has any sympathy for me?" We do. I talked about this in an earlier chapter—men are frequently the victims of domestic violence. Many victims have messaged the podcast and told me how they were hit or abused in some fashion. Is it not wrong when domestic violence happens to these men? Why are they not on billboards? Why isn't anybody listening to them? Well, we're listening.

The data shows millions of men are the victims of domestic violence, but I'd bet it's much higher than anyone really knows, because the majority of guys are too ashamed to report it. So, they're not reflected in the statistics.

I've heard from abused dads who've tried to go to a domestic violence shelter only to be turned away because they're men. One guy, a veteran, said his wife was relentlessly beating him and their children and forcing them to sleep on the floor. One day he took his children and left. He went to five different shelters, and all five turned him away. They told him they didn't take men since men were the ones who abused the women staying there. So, where is this guy supposed to go with his kids? Do you know how many domestic violence shelters exist for men? You can count them on the fingers of one hand.

A sad part of this is how it very clearly affects the children. Often the kids will end up living with the abuser. Then Dad has to interact with the abuser every time he goes over to see his children. In most states, the family court system gives the woman the power. If Dad threatens to report Mom, she'll withhold visitation. Custodial interference is a crime but if the mother blocks the dad, the system won't do anything about it. Where does that guy go? Nobody listens. Well, we do. Band together let's rebuild the system together.

Remember that dad named Robert who I mentioned earlier who talked about how he'd suffered parental alienation? He later shared the importance of finding resources. "I did actually try to look for resources, not only as a veteran but just as a man, you know, I tried to see if there were any organizations like domestic violence-related or anything that could provide me support in what I was going through, and quite frankly I had extreme difficulty finding anything whatsoever that was of any support." Robert did end up being helped by the Wounded Warrior

Project. They led him to a program that helped him get therapy, which he said helped significantly.

At the risk of coming off like I'm in a pitch meeting for *Dad Talk Today*, I want frustrated and hurting dads to know you are welcome there. It's your space—a community where dads share their stories, their hurts, their challenges, and yes, even their victories. A lot of dads listen or watch and never participate because they're either ashamed or afraid whatever they share will be used against them. Think about that. Guys are afraid to talk about what's ailing them because their emotions could be used against them. They're going through some of the toughest battles a man can face. When someone messes with a man's family, they're messing with a man's existence.

So, what I'm wanting to do with *Dad Talk Today* is to reach that guy sitting in his home all alone who thinks he has nothing left to give. I was you five or six years ago. You do matter. Where do hurting guys go? Come here. Come here and speak up. Let's work together to facilitate change.

See, when you go to these people—your legislators—to talk about changing things, they always say, "Oh, you need to keep the focus on the children. It's not about the dads." Oh, you think?! Of course, I'm focused on my children! That's why I am doing this! Then they'll say it's not about the money. They use smoke and mirrors to keep you from trying to change anything. They don't want you talking about it. Here's why—because when you guys come together and get out the real message of how the system puts a price tag on families, it threatens livelihoods. Here's what I would ask a family law lawyer or a legislator—why does a guy have to pay to be a dad? Why doesn't he have equal parental rights from the second his child is born? Why doesn't he have equal rights to his child if the relationship with the kid's mother goes south?

Men will show up to work even when they're hurting. Men are, by nature, providers and protectors, and that's why they often get screwed. Even though a dad might feel defeated, he keeps feeding the system because he will do anything to stay in his family's life. Society has convinced men that the more they love their children, the more they will pay.

We have a problem. Clearly. We need every single dad right now. Hurting dads, use that pain to help fuel the movement. Join us at *Dad Talk Today*. There's strength in volume. Realistically, if you go to the courts, you'll get nothing. If you tell the media, you'll get nothing. If you sit at home alone, you'll get depression and an empty wallet. But if you gather with like-minded dads, you'll likely hear a message that makes you say, "I've been feeling like that guy, and I want to get involved. I want people to know my story." And your story will often help another guy.

But it's not just about the individual story. It's about a million stories. Their collective power can't be ignored. Look, I spent four years attending political conferences and roundtables, and for what? Let me tell you what happens when you try to sound the alarm with people who have the ability to make a difference—it gets worse. Because when they recognize you're trying to bring awareness to the inequities in the system, they'll push legislation to make it even harder for you. Oh, I'll admit we found way more support with national politicians, celebrities, and many powerful people than I could have imagined. We've made some inroads in terms of the effort to change legislation—not a ton, but we've been asking a whole lot of people, "Why isn't anybody doing anything?" But this movement for hurting dads has to get bigger. More of us have to be out there saying, "Enough with the bogus narratives!"

Guys, a lot of you are hurting. But let's get together and change the world. We have to get crazy—maybe not literally, but people think we're crazy for thinking we can change things. People will accuse you of wearing a tinfoil hat for saying the system is biased against dads. Ignore them. You're not. Maybe doing the things they say are crazy are actually the sane things required to force change to a system nobody thinks can be changed. Let's get crazy, guys —crazy enough to think we can change the world—because we can.

Some people think dads are disposable. Commodities. It feels like that for some of us, especially when you're going through a divorce and the ensuing custody issues, and you don't feel like you've got anyone to talk to. I felt that way. Ever heard of the "divorce diet?" I lost 60 pounds in about three months. I wasn't eating. I wasn't sleeping. I was worried about my family. I cried my eyes out when nobody was around. I felt lifeless and didn't want to exist. I just wanted my family. Even so, I powered through and kept going to work—just like most of you did. But it's my belief that's the last place a guy going through this should be. He has to get help—counseling or some sort of therapeutic resource. Some employers do offer those programs because they know you'll be a better employee in the long run. But then again, on the flip side of that is the stigma—a lot of dads won't go to counseling because it's often used against them in court. So, of course, that makes a hurting dad feel even more alone.

One of the best, most effective therapies I've seen for men costs nothing. It's talk—a space with supportive people, where they can say what's on their mind—with people who can relate without judgment; a place where people will listen, and a hurting dad will know their words won't be used against them. We need no judgment zones. Meantime, that's *Dad Talk Today*. No judgment there. I sincerely believe dads can relate to other dads.

Any hurting dad can hit up the comment section of the podcast. Talk to each other. Introduce yourselves and share what you've been through, and what you're dealing with now. You'd be amazed at the number of guys who share your experience. It's part and parcel of building a community—a community where hurting dads can get comfort, and that can, and will, change the world.

TWELVE
WE'RE AT WAR

AMERICA IS FIGHTING A WAR—not with Russia, not with China, not with North Korea. The war is within. And the war within our particular corner of the world—the family court system—feels a lot like the Alamo under siege by Santa Anna's army.

The system weaponizes everything. You've been blocked by custodial interference. You've not been allowed to see your kids. You've had your holidays blocked. You've been on the other end of false allegations. And what resources to fight back do you really have?

We are at war.

You take away somebody's kids; you take away their livelihood, reputation, and money and what do you think that does to their thinking? If a dad hadn't been through it before, you think their perspective might change, now? Damn right it would. Only then does one truly appreciate how unfair and truly crooked the system is. How many times have I heard from a politician who said, "I've looked into the issues and yes, it's definitely unfair." Yeah? Well, where were you when I was asking *you* for help? I'll tell you where you were—you were pushing the conversation about abortion. You were talking about drag shows. You were talking about Ukraine. You were talking about the economy. You were talking about climate change. You were talking about the border. You were talking about anything and everything except the biased family court system.

Increasingly, we're the ones forcing the conversation.

Sometimes, it's just plain exhausting. It's easy to get complacent. There are a lot of guys who just can't battle anymore. I know what that's like. It's no wonder we get worn to the nub. I mean, who does a dad have to talk to? Where are his resources? If a guy falls behind on child support, where does he go for help? But to the guy who has been beaten down and battered I say, come back! I know you've had many promises. I know you're tired of the fight. But we've got to keep on hanging in there, Dad. We're up against villainy. Your kids' lives are at stake, your grand-kids', too. Let's fix it for them. Let's fix it for the next generation of dads.

We're facing evil. I mean, what else would you call anything that denies a father a right to his kids? And, if you don't think it's getting worse, you're not paying attention. If we fail to rise up now, then we fail our kids. And if we can't change the policies of today, then where are we going to be tomorrow? We're dangerously close to not being able to put the genie back in the bottle. There is no time for messing around. None.

We need to rise up and fight for the rights that were given to us by God. A court doesn't get to "allow" us to be a dad. Lawyers don't dictate whether I get to be a father to my kids.

We need to get our army together. You dads are out there. I've met you. I've heard from you. You call in. You listen. You're there in numbers. And I'm here for you. *Dad Talk Today* exists to equip you with a platform for support and reinforcement. Dads fight tooth and nail for custody equity. But many of them are so gaslit by the system and the lawyers and the exes that eventually they start thinking, "Maybe it's my fault." "I need to be a better person." They beat themselves up because it feels like nobody's listening to them. They can't get resolution. Still others are the target of false allegations or they're alienated from their kids, which is undoubtedly followed by guilt—"Did I do everything I could?" It's unfair.

Don't fall into that trap. We're in a war, and, yes, the battles will exhaust the hell out of you, but stick it out. Be in it to win it. The research is on our side, guys, we've just got to get it out there. Your stories are what empowers that.

Your pain isn't in vain. There is a reason. There is a purpose, and you can turn that pain into purpose. I believe this is the generation that can make the change. If dads simply get together and show up and speak up.

You want to know how to fight against this; how to fight against this system? It begins with changing the narrative. We've got to change the culture. Having the kids go to the mother shouldn't be the default setting in custody cases. There are three sides to these cases— his side, her side, and the truth. But it seems the only side that ever matters is the mother's.

Don't empower the other side by giving them anything

that discredits you. Be it a shortage of time or money, or any manner of challenges, whatever you're going through they will use against you. You could say one hundred things and they'll grab hold of one little thing they can use to discredit you. They can make any allegation and these days you won't be believed. You could lose everything.

I'm trying hard to train the frustrated dad. I've got a podcast on social media platforms, which, truth be told, I look at it like a boot camp. We're building an army of dads —dads who'll effectively fight back against a biased system. And don't misinterpret what I'm saying, this isn't a physical fight. It's a fight to change the narrative.

It's an oft-confusing time. Imagine you're in court and the judge talks about, "the best interests of the child," yet when you ask any judge to define it, you never get a consistent answer. Ask different, so-called experts, "What's parental alienation?" You'll get a myriad of answers. And candidly, what does equality even mean anymore? I don't have the answers. I'm not an attorney. I don't want to be an attorney. I'm the last person on Earth who is going to tell you how to fight your court case. I'm not here to give anyone legal advice. There are plenty of people out there who can do that. But I'm a guy rallying the troops—saying, let's get together, let's get educated, let's be empowered, and let's win this thing.

We need leaders in this movement who'll work at their local and state levels. Find thought leaders who'll educate dads on how to navigate CPS, child support issues, alimony issues, or how to represent themselves in court, which is called "pro se." From custody exchanges to false allegations to sexual abuse allegations to domestic violence allegations, dads need educational support groups to help them with a plan of action in every area. What may seem small at first ultimately becomes a full-fledged network of help, support, and resources.

Don't let the Neanderthal opposition stop or discourage you. Oh, they'll try, especially when you start talking sense. The more sensible your points, the greater the pushback. Expect it. Prepare for it. I've been through it. The bigger my podcast gets, the harder they come. I was once falsely accused of generating hundreds of thousands of dollars with the podcast and amassing a multimillion dollar net worth. All of it was untrue—just outright defamation. You have to see through that. You have to see their motivation. They spread those lies so dads would stop contributing. They're desperate to stop the movement, by all means necessary. Don't you let 'em!

I know you're frustrated. Truth be told, I've wanted to quit many times—to just throw in the towel. Some days it's so disheartening to hear story after story from dads mistreated in all manner of ways. Candidly, it feels like we're fighting a losing battle. The opposition has a plan, and they execute it without remorse. But we are not fighting a losing battle. The battle can and will be won! And that's why I'm not going anywhere... and neither should you.

CONCLUSION

Look, guys, I'd love to sell you the idea we're going to win this thing tomorrow—that we'll win the culture war, beat back the false narratives, change the family court system, and end the behemoth government grift called "child support." But that ain't happening tomorrow. But I do believe if we keep this going and doing what we're doing, it will happen. We're fighting a multibillion dollar a year industry, and people just don't realize it really is David versus Goliath. It feels like we're throwing rocks at people who have machine guns. And they are organized.

This fight reminds me of *The Lord of the Rings*. That sounds crazy, right? But the family court, it's the Precious— it's what makes the money and keeps the industry going. The false allegations, conflict, bias, and the narrative—all of these things make the Precious the family court. But I want you to think about Sméagol. He seemed like such a good guy, didn't he? At first. So, Frodo gets in there and gets the ring. Sméagol is like, "No, you don't touch my Precious!"

If you're not familiar with *The Lord of the Rings*, Precious is a name given to the One Ring—as described by one fan blog, which describes it best, the use of the name indicates "the morbid covetousness induced in holders of the Ring by the Ring itself."[1] Few things describe the family court system and the industry around it better than "morbid covetousness."

The average dad going through the system—he's worried. "Where's my wife? Where are my kids? Are my kids being abused? Are they calling somebody else, 'Daddy?' I don't have any money. Do I work my overtime today? What little money I have, do I give it to a lawyer? How do I fight get the rights to my kids, and why do I even have to fight for them to begin with? When did I give the government the right to give me permission on when, where, and how I see my kids?"

There are lot of dads experiencing the problems in family court—the bias and the narrative, but when you start talking about completely annihilating the system, that's when Sméagol comes out, and he has to protect the Precious, at all costs. He's going to protect his industry. He's going to protect his money.

Guys, we need to be talking about getting rid of this system completely. There are guys in the middle of this right now and they need some help. They need strategy. They wonder, "How do I do this?" One thing I would say to the dad community—I've met a lot of guys who didn't hire attorneys, they represented themselves and they wiped the floor with the attorneys fighting them. You want to know how to fight against this—how to fight against this system? Get informed. Knowledge is power. We've got to change the narrative. We've got to change the culture.

I'll confess, some days it's hard to stay the course. It's easy to be overwhelmed by the sheer volume of tragic stories. I'll sit before the microphone and question whether what I say makes a difference. I question whether anyone relates. I wonder how people will react. I'll sit there wondering is it okay for me to talk about this? But what makes it worth it is when a guy reacts and says, "Yes, that's my situation!" That's the moment it becomes real. There are real human beings struggling through seemingly insurmountable challenges.

Can it be depressing at times? Yes, it can, but it's real. We all have our respective challenges. It would be nice to be able to share those with other empathetic dads without judgment. Men don't really have a place to vent. When I started *Dad Talk Today* I told myself I wanted to make a difference, to hell with being a popular page. Funny thing is it actually became pretty popular. I've tried to be transparent. I've shared things that were good to share. Others, not so much. But one thing I will never regret is taking a stand for dads. If we truly want to make a difference we cannot skip over the hurt. We can't bury it. We have to use it to spur change.

My ultimate goal in the very beginning was to shed some light on the bias that exists in family court. For anybody who says there's not a bias against men in family court, you're not only lying to yourself, but to everyone else, too. The system is broken, it's been broken for many years, and many of these men are doing everything they can to hold on so they can be here for their children. That's the truth regardless of whether you choose to believe it.

Dad, think about what you're facing—what you're

going through. Is it a financial struggle? Is it grief? Have you been trying to be a parent instead of a friend and not succeeding? Are you battling negative societal narratives about fathers? Maybe you're just learning how to potty train the kid or how to dress them for school. Man, I have experienced all of those things and more.

I started a voicemail line so that we could hear from you. Guys, there are so many of us going through similar challenges. The only way the system will ever change is when you speak up. I can get on a podcast every day and blast it out over every social media platform, but I'm just a lone ranger. I'm one of you—just another dad. We need to be a collective voice. Strength in numbers.

Being a dad is a special calling. It's life-changing. When I became a dad for the first time, I grew up. I mean, it just snapped me out of my immaturity and forced me into becoming a man. Before fatherhood, I was an immature guy trying to find his way who spent all his time driving fast and listening to Metallica at full volume... although even mature dads still do that. Lord knows I do! Seriously though, becoming a father molded me into who I am today. Just who am I? I'm a man who's made more than his share of mistakes, but one who isn't embarrassed to talk about them because I hope it encourages other men to speak.

Maybe I'm just a dreamer, but Martin Luther King had a dream, too. His dream created a civil rights movement that changed history. Dads need a history-changing movement of their own. Imagine if Dr. King had been marching alone? There'd be no change. So, dads, don't march alone. There are more of us than you might even realize! And if you need a mantra, a clarion call for the movement, look no further than this song by The Doors called "Five to One"—

The old get old, and the young get stronger
May take a week, and it may take longer
They got the guns, well, but we got the numbers
Gonna win, yeah, we're takin' over

I promise you, we're gonna win. It might not be tomorrow; it might take longer. But we will win. They may have the guns, but we've got the numbers. Dads, we're taking over.

AFP

ACKNOWLEDGMENTS

Whether it's producing a podcast or writing a book, I couldn't accomplish a thing without some extraordinarily special people.

First, my wife is my everything. People might think that because of what I'm doing—fighting for the rights of men and dads—that I'm anti-woman or anti-marriage, well, that couldn't be further from the truth. My wife makes it possible for me to do what I do. If it wasn't for her, I wouldn't be doing *Dad Talk Today*. I love my wife more than anything on the face of this earth. She is my rock. She is my pillar. When I've wanted to give up she's been the one helping me to continue. She knows this is my passion and my heart, and because she truly is here to support me, she supports everything about me. My wife has never tried to get me to conform to what she wants, she allows me to be me. To my wife, thank you so much for believing in me because there aren't too many women who would have put up with everything I do. You mean the world to me.

My dad—what can I say about such an incredible man? I lost my dad in 2013. He was a pastor, and he was the one who showed me what it means to want to help people. I think a lot of people help others just to signal their virtue, you know, "Look at what I'm doing for the world." But Dad was never like that. He was always doing things for other people. It didn't matter whether people appreciated what he did, he still did it. My dad gave to others for all the right reasons. He never took a salary as a pastor. He did the work because he genuinely liked helping people. He knew more about the meaning of life than I ever did... or will. Even though he isn't here anymore, I'm still learning from him. The wisdom that I have and the lessons I teach my own children, I only have because I was his son. When I think about what my life would've been like without my father, I shudder to consider where I'd be right now. So, to you, big man, I love you and I miss you more than anything in this world.

My mom has been a huge pillar of support through every up and every down. She's been there through my not-so-pretty years and even now, through every peak and valley. I can't tell her enough how much I love her and how proud I am of her for taking control since my dad passed away. I'm proud to be my mother's son.

To all four of my children—I love you so much. I am proud of each of you and my love for you is unconditional. I will always be there for you regardless of whatever you do in life. You might not understand what your dad is doing with this *Dad Talk* thing right now, but I believe in due time you will.

To my daughter who I haven't seen since she was a year old, please know that I love you so much. But because of the rigged family court system, I'm unable to see you. But know that it's because of my love for you and desire to be in your life that I wake up every single day thinking of you —and whether it's this book or my podcast, the thought of you is what keeps me going when I want to quit. I hope that one day you'll see what your dad has done and realize it was all for you. I won't become another statistic and I am sorry you are losing this time with your father. But know there's not a day that goes by that I'm not fighting for you, as well as for other children who find themselves in the same situation.

Thank you to everybody who has ever supported *Dad Talk Today*. I couldn't have done any of this without you.

I want to thank so many people, but I sure wouldn't want to leave anyone out. You know who you are and I appreciate each of you. Hopefully I've let you know this on a personal level every step of the way.

To my mentors, to my publisher Dan, and to the people who have been in this movement for years that have taken me under their wing and given me knowledge, thank you. I have more respect for you sitting here today than I did when I started. I didn't know how much work this would be—and at first I didn't fully appreciate the thankless work you've done trying to create change, but I do now.

I love and appreciate you all.

ABOUT THE AUTHOR

Eric Carroll is the founder and host of *Dad Talk Today*—a podcast that raises awareness of the challenges faced by fathers in the family court system and provides information and resources to help them face the challenges. *Dad Talk Today* has grown a following to over one million people across a variety of social media platforms.

Eric himself is a father engaged in fighting the broken family court system—the system that prevented him from seeing his first-born daughter.

Though *Dad Talk Today* has grown to be a successful endeavor and has allowed Eric the opportunity to visit over 40 states and to interview all manner of celebrities and politicians, the thing he cares most about is his family.

Eric loves being a husband. He loves being a father. He's a fan of classic cars, classic rock, and being a family man.

Eric is the father of four beautiful children.

[f] facebook.com/dadtalktoday

[X] x.com/dadtalktoday

[O] instagram.com/dadtalktoday

[♪] tiktok.com/@dadtalktoday1

NOTES

INTRODUCTION

1. United States Census Bureau, "America's Families and Living Arrangements: 2021," Table C2, November 29, 2021, https://www.census.gov/data/tables/2021/demo/families/cps-2021.html

3. GUILTY UNTIL PROVEN INNOCENT

1. Brown, Edward. "Fatherhood Under Attack?" *Fort Worth Weekly*, February 8, 2023
2. Ibid

4. THE WAR ON MASCULINITY

1. Vallie, Sarah. "What Is Toxic Masculinity?" WebMD, November 11, 2022
2. Thompson, Akola. "Are all men toxic?" The Minority Report, *Stabroek News*, September 23, 2022
3. Salter, Michael. "The Problem with a Fight Against Toxic Masculinity" *The Atlantic*, February 27, 2019
4. "National Strategy on Gender Equity and Equality." The White House Gender Policy Council, March 2021. https://www.whitehouse.gov/wp-content/uploads/2021/10/National-Strategy-on-Gender-Equity-and-Equality.pdf

5. HOW SOCIETY ATTACKS MEN AND DADS

1. Ruth W. Leemis, Norah Friar, Srijana Khatiwada, May S. Chen, Marcie-jo Kresnow, Sharon G. Smith, Sharon Caslin, and Kathleen C. Basile. "The National Intimate Partner and Sexual Violence Survey: 2016/2017 Report on Intimate Partner Violence." Centers for Disease Control and Prevention, October 2022

2. Martin, Tom. "You can't deny it. Gender studies is full of male-blaming bias." *The Guardian*, September 14, 2011

7. THE FATHERLESS ISSUE

1. Lydia R. Anderson, Paul F. Hemez, and Rose M. Kreider. "Living Arrangements of Children: 2019" US Census Bureau, Washington, DC
2. Office of the Assistant Secretary for Planning and Evaluation. *ASPE Issue Brief*, US Department of Health and Human Services, September 11, 2012
3. National Fatherhood Initiative 2019. "Father Facts: Eighth Edition." Germantown, MD
4. Bendheim-Thomas Center for Research on Child Wellbeing and Social Indicators Survey Center. "CPS involvement in families with social fathers. Fragile Families Research Brief." 2010
5. National Fatherhood Initiative 2019. "Father Facts: Eighth Edition." Germantown, MD
6. Allen, A. N., & Lo, C. C. "Drugs, guns, and disadvantaged youths: Co-occurring behavior and the code of the street." *Crime & Delinquency*, 2012
7. Adamsons, K., & Johnson, S. K. "An updated and expanded meta-analysis of nonresident fathering and child well-being." *Journal of Family Psychology*, 2013
8. Bendheim-Thomas Center for Research on Child Wellbeing and Social Indicators Survey Center. "CPS involvement in families with social fathers. Fragile Families Research Brief." 2010
9. Whitney, S., Prewett, S., Wang, Ze, & Haigin C. "Fathers' importance in adolescents' academic achievement." *International Journal of Child, Youth and Family Studies*, 2017
10. Affuso, G., Bacchini, D., Miranda, M.C. "The contribution of school-related parental monitoring, self-determination, and self-efficacy to academic achievement." *The Journal of Educational Research*, 2017
11. Whitney, S., Prewett, S., Wang, Ze, & Haigin C. "Fathers' importance in adolescents' academic achievement." *International Journal of Child, Youth and Family Studies*, 2017
12. Grossbard, Shoshana (Editor), *Marriage and the Economy: Theory and Evidence from Advanced Industrial Societies*, 2003
13. Peterson, P.E. "Government Should Subsidize, Not Tax, Marriage: Social policies have influenced the rate of growth in single-parent families." *Education Next*, 15(2), 64-68, 2015

8. WHY ARE DADS DENIED EQUAL PARENTING?

1. https://www.transparencyusa.org/tx/candidate/victoria-neave-coh/ Accessed January 8, 2023
2. Bauserman, Dr. Robert. "Child Adjustment in Joint-Custody Versus Sole-Custody Arrangements: A Meta-Analytic Review." *Journal of Family Psychology*, Volume 16, Number 1, 2002

9. HOW THE CHILD SUPPORT SYSTEM IS BROKEN

1. State Financing of Child Support Enforcement Programs. Final Report. Contract Number 100-96-0011. Prepared for: Assistant Secretary for Planning and Evaluation and Office of Child Support Enforcement Department of Health and Human Services
2. Cimini, Kate. "California keeps millions in child support while parents drown in debt." *CalMatters*, May 3, 2021

10. EVERY OTHER WEEKEND ISN'T ENOUGH

1. Pierson, Lacie. "W. Va.'s 50-50 custody law now in effect." *The Herald-Dispatch*, June 11, 2022

CONCLUSION

1. Tolkien Gateway. https://Tolkengateway.net/wiki/Precious. Accessed April 16, 2023

INDEX

Beavis and Butt-Head Do the Universe (film), 41–42

Beavis and Butt-Head (television series, old and new), 41

"Best Interests of the Child Protection Act"

   (West Virginia), 77–78

bias against men, causes of, 25

Bible, quoted, 85

Biden administration, 27–29

Bond, James (old and new), 27

Bowlby, Dr. John, 72–73

brotherhood, need for, 7–9

Buc-ee's, 21

"build back better," 27

bulletproof vests, 12

C

California, takes 14% of child support payments, 63

camera, should one film exchanges?, 12

cancel culture, 70

cancer, child dying of, a terrible example, xxi–xxiii

Carson, Dr. Ben, 48–49

CDC (Centers for Disease Control and Prevention), 28, 33

children

   often figure out who's right as they get older, 5

   suffer the most, 7

child support, 62–71

   father's need to earn more cuts into time with kids, 67–69

   mothers often spend it on themselves, 65

   not adjusted for expense of joint custody, 71

   often adjusted upward, rarely downward, 65–66

   often supports ex's new family, 63, 68

   only really benefits lawyers, 64

informed, importance of being, 98
innocent until proven guilty, everyone except a
　　　divorced dad, 15
International Journal of Child, Youth and Family Studies, 46–47
isolation, as an ex's tactic, 84

J

John Mast Foundation, 17
Johnson, Lyndon B., 49
joint custody, healthier for kids than sole custody, 60-61
Jorgensen, Jo, 47
journalists, activists disguised as, 29
Journal of Family Psychology, 60–61
Judeo-Christian values, 50
jury of peers, not found in family court, 57

K

The Karate Kid (film), 38–39
Kennedy, John F., 49
King, Dr. Martin Luther, Jr., 50–51, 100

L

laws, state, you must know them, 6
lawyers
　basically snakes in disguise, xviii
　despicable, 78
　exceptions, not all are shady, 16–17
　only ones who profit from child support system, 64
　profit from conflict, 16
　some can win without them, 98
Leave it to Beaver, 32